Tennis
2200405

CHRONOSPORTS
E D I T E U R

For French Edition:
ISBN 2-84707-077-X

For English Edition:
ISBN 2-84707-068-0

© Decembre 2004, Chronosports S.A.
Jordils Park, Chemin des Jordils 40, CH-1025 St-Sulpice, Switzerland.
Tél: (+41 21) 694 24 44.
Fax: (+41 21) 694 24 46.
E-mail: info@chronosports.com
www.chronosports.com

Printed in France by Imprimerie Clerc.
Bound in France by S.I.R.C.

Tennis
2004/05

Words
Philippe Callewaert

Translate from French
Natacha De Roeck

Design
Sabrina Favre

Illustrations
Cyril Davillerd

Layout
Sabrina Favre

Coordination
Sabrina Favre

Results
Solange Amara, Sabrina Favre

Photos
Agence France Presse (AFP)

Table of Contents

8 End 2003 – Summary

14 Roger Federer

22 Australian Open

38 Davis Cup (1st round)

40 Tokyo (WTA)

42 Indian Wells (ATP/WTA)

46 Serena Williams

52 Miami (ATP/WTA)

56 Davis Cup (2nd round)

58 Charleston (WTA)

60 Monte-Carlo (ATP)

62 Fed Cup (1st round)

64 Rome (ATP)

66 Berlin (WTA)

68 Hambourg (ATP)

70 Rome (WTA)

74 Roland-Garros

92 The Russians' Year

100 Wimbledon

118 Fed Cup (2nd round)

120 Toronto (WTA)

122 San Diego (WTA)

124 Cincinnati (ATP)

126 Montreal (ATP)

130 Justine Henin-Hardenne

134 Olympic Games of Athens

144 Amélie Mauresmo

152 US Open

168 Davis Cup (Semifinals)

170 Gaël Monfils

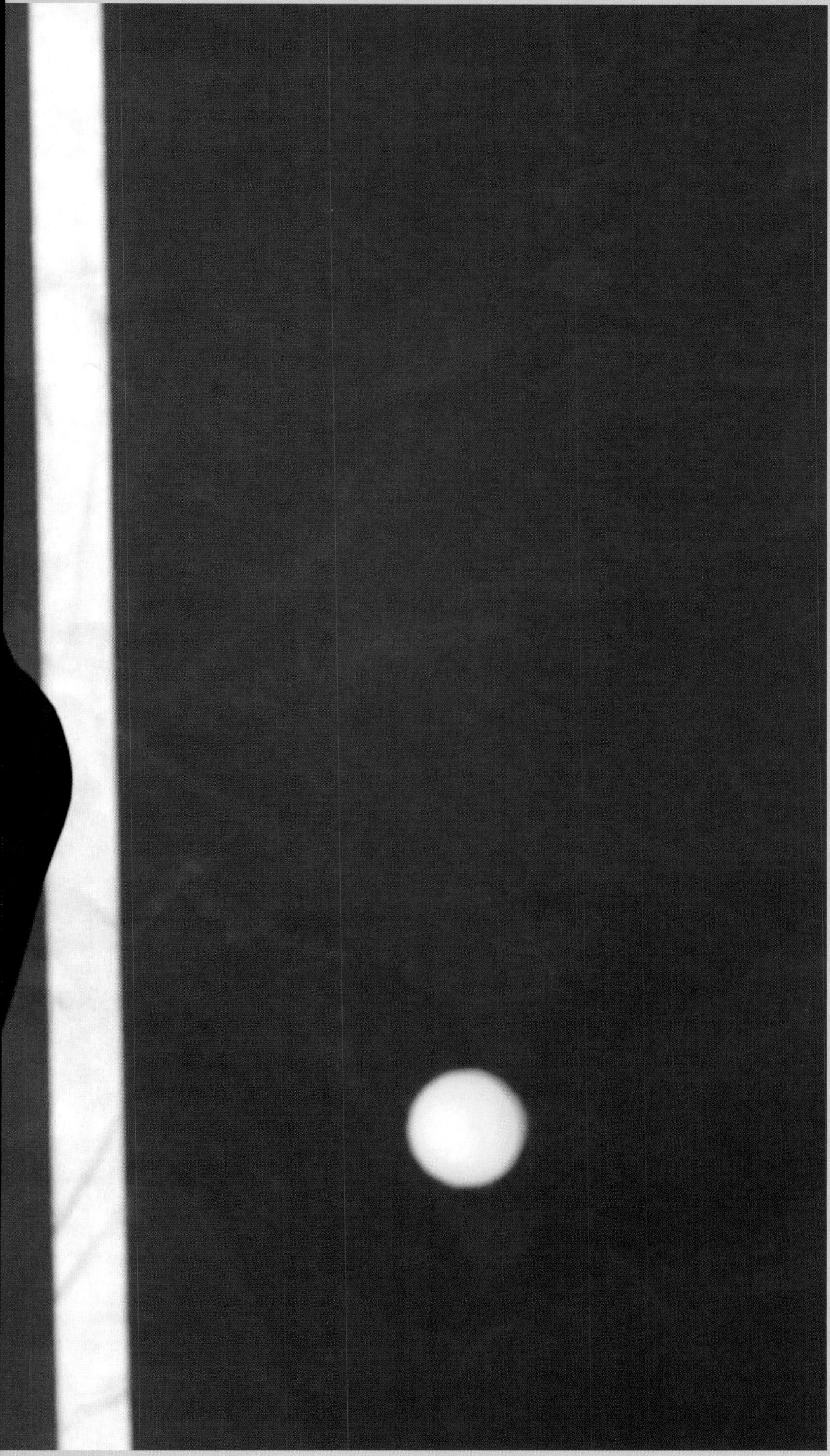

Remember 2003!

One Day to Remember in 2003...

August 25, 2003 – a historical date. The American tennis player Pete Sampras officially retires from competition.

He is then 'only' 32 years old. The only man who has won a record fourteen Grand Slam singles titles chooses Arthur Ashe Stadium in Flushing Meadows of the US Open 2003 to announce his retirement. This day marks the end of an era in tennis history. There was a time 'before' Pete Sampras and there now is a time 'after' him.

2003 ATP Race

Andy Roddick Playing his "A" Game

In addition to the above-mentioned event, one has to remember mainly four Grand Slam victories: those of Andre Agassi in Melbourne, Juan Carlos Ferrero in Roland-Garros, Roger Federer in Wimbledon and Andy Roddick at the US Open. These 4 winners are therefore the 4 greatest players of the year, as well as the first 4 seeded at the end of the Race. 21-years-old Andy Roddick becomes the youngest American to be World No. 1. In 2003, he won six titles, including the US Open, i.e. 72 victories against only 19 defeats. A few points behind him, the Swiss Roger Federer hardly starts showing his brightness. Fight between those two players will make the 2004 Race joyfully attractive. However, the Wimbledon champion seems to be a few steps ahead. Andre Agassi's fourth rank is even more spectacular if we compare his age with the top 3 players (eg, Juan Carlos Ferrero, No. 3 is 10 years younger than him). The 2003 Race also makes the American player the oldest No. 1 in history and the oldest Masters Cup finalist since Arthur Ashe in 1978. Not too bad.

On the left:
Pete Sampras   Andy Roddick

3 For the first time since ATP ranking creation in 1973, the world ranking has been totally renewed from one year to another. In 2003, the names of Roddick, Federer and Ferrero replaced those of Hewitt, Agassi and Safin on the top 3 chart.

Roger Federer

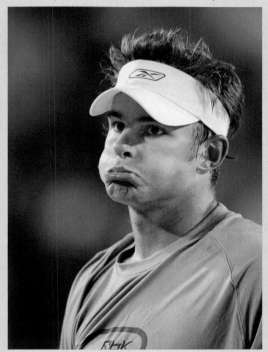

" I never thought of being No. 1 when I was younger. It has never even been on my mind. When I was 12, I could hardly lace up my shoes. "

Andy Roddick,
2003 World No.1.

Masters Cup, November 2003

Roger Federer Announces his Ambitions for 2004

Houston, USA. The first 8 ATP players meet at Westside Tennis Club to fight for the last ATP tournament of the year, the Masters Cup. It is a good opportunity for them to face each other for the last time before well-deserved holidays. Houston is filled with an Italian far west movie atmosphere. Organizers did utmost to give a great opening ceremony. Protagonists of the week appeared wearing local clothes, suits and ties, and elegant Stetson hats. The show may start. Ladies and Gentlemen, we are glad to introduce you first ranking players with, in the main roles, Mr Andy Roddick (recent No. 1 of the Race since the Paris-Bercy Masters Series), Mr Juan Carlos Ferrero (slightly weakened by a knuckle injury), Mr Roger Federer (in very good shape in spite of some dorsal pain), Mr Guillermo Coria (like all Argentines less at ease on such a surface), Mr Andre Agassi (the oldest participant of a Masters' final), Mr Rainer Schuettler (with 97 victories this year), Mr Carlos Moya (who celebrates his fourth Masters Cup's qualification) and last but not least, Mr David Nalbandian (for his first Masters Cup). The winning hero of the play comes from Switzerland and his name is Roger Federer. He came in Houston to make his job –as he said – and he claimed his seventh success of the season, winning US$ 1.5 million (reaching a total amount of US$ 4 million this year). The hero could have been Spanish but destiny decided otherwise as Juan Carlos Ferrero failed to take Andy Roddick's first place. Andre Agassi could only be astonished by an imperial Federer in the final. The American was literally crushed by the young Swiss, who won a 6-3, 6-0, 6-4 victory. "There is nothing to be done when he plays such a way", he explained at the end of the match. Was tiredness Schuetller's main enemy? Guillermo Coria would have preferred to play on clay but it did not prevent him from winning at least one match during 'robin round' against Carlos Moya. His fellow David Nalbandian did just the same. Only Andy Roddick left Texas ground with great satisfaction, i.e. with the title of World champion, even if he was defeated in the semi-finals by Federer. The end.

2003 WTA season

Justine Henin-Hardenne: Best of Belgians, Best of the World.

An extraordinary season. It started like the previous one had ended, meaning, under the Williams sisters' supremacy as they both were once again finalists in a Grand Slam. The face to face at the Australian Open finally completed on a Serena's victory. This kind of screenplay had already been shot in the past since it was the fourht time they met in a Grand Slam final. However, few months later, Women tennis becomes an amazing plot, coming from Belgium. Most of Williams' supporters are first unable to spot this country on a world map. But then, thanks to Justine Henin-Hardenne and Kim Clijsters's high levels and thanks to all the tournaments they win, everybody starts hearing about the small country. For Justine, the best tournament is and will remain Paris. Although everybody is betting on another Williams victory, Justine breaks some kind of monotony, becoming the first Belgian tennis player (men and women) to win such a great tournament. The screenplay would not have been so crusty, had not the other finalist been her fellow Kim Clijsters. We were to witness the first 100% Belgian final in a Grand Slam tournament ever. June 7, 2003 – beginning of a great fighting game between the Flemish and the Walloon girls. Both of them are successively World No. 1. Kim is No. 1, even without having won any Grand Slam's champion title in her career. But at the end of the Tour, she holds 9 titles (19 in her full career). After a new champion title at Wimbledon for Serena Williams, again playing her sister, both of them have to withdraw from end-year competition due to repeated injuries. Those health troubles allow the two Belgian players to meet again in the final of one of the four biggest tournaments, Flushing Meadows. Justine Henin-Hardenne captures a second Grand Slam title, honoured by a World No. 1 ranking at the end of 2003.

Justine Henin-Hardenne

November 2003 - Women's Masters

Second is Best

A big paycheck. As winner of the WTA Tour Championships, the Belgian player Kim Clijsters made the best money of all players. Meaning US$ 1.000.030. The last US$ 30 are symbolic. They represent the 30th anniversary of WTA tour. Never mind the US$ 30, the world second-seeded ends the 2003 season with an amount of US$ 4.091.591 to add to her bank account. This money was collected in single and double matches. It is the biggest amount ever earned by a sportswoman in one single year.
At Staples Centre in Los Angeles, sacred temple of basketball teams of the Clippers and the Lakers, Kim Clijsters wins her ninth title of the year, the women's Masters, considered as the most important event after Grand Slam's tournaments. This year, this event takes a new form. Instead of the usual tables with direct elimination gathering the 16 best players in the world, there are only eight of them (Kim Clijsters, Justine Henin-Hardenne, Jennifer Capriati, Amelie Mauresmo, Anastasia Myskina, Elena Dementieva, Ai Sugiyama and Chanda Rubin) facing each other in two pools of four players each. It is actually the same as for Men's Master Cup. The best two players of each pool then meet in the semi-finals.
Kindly note the absence of Williams sisters and Lindsay Davenport due to injuries. Californian audience is going to attend a final between the French Amelie Mauresmo and the Belgian Kim Clijsters. The latter defeated Jennifer Capriati while Amelie was beating World No. 1 in semi-finals and therefore becoming the second French woman to attend a Masters final after Mary Pierce in 1997. However, it would be better to forget this final match rather quickly, since Mauresmo won only two games in front of the defending champion (6/2, 6/0). A pity for the French player, extraordinary for the Belgian one: out of two events, she won the nine singles she played. "I played my best match of the year, she concludes. Today the ball felt like a football. It is always very pleasant to know that you can do everything you wish with it."

2003 Fed Cup

A team victory

OK, USA was deprived of both Williams sisters, so Davenport, Capriati and Belgium had to 'manage' without the best two world champions. OK, but even so! Sunday November 23, 2003 – a key-date in French tennis' history. In Moscow, Female French team wins Fed Cup's final for the second time in history (defeating USA). Thanks to this victory, Guy Forget manages as well as Yannick Noah in 1997 and becomes the second French Captain to win both Davis Cup and Fed Cup.
This competition's form slightly differs from Davis Cup's. Final steps (semi- and final) take place during the same week. Therefore, from November 17 until 23, there are two sides: USA vs Belgium and France vs Russia. This last mentioned match already looks like a real final. It is the most attractive meeting of the week. Indeed, all of the female players in the Russian team were attending Los Angeles Masters the week before: Myskina, Dementieva, Petrova and Zvonareva. The mission, for Amelie Mauresmo, Mary Pierce, Emilie Loit and Stephanie Cohen-Aloro is therefore not that easy. However... they take great benefit from their captain's knowledge: trust, sense of risk and talent. Guy Forget brightly takes his league captain responsibilities, reinstating a top-levelled Mary Pierce as team No. 2 instead of Nathalie Dechy, whose fist is injured. Pierce is then stepping back into the France team, she had left it in 1997. It was a Fed Cup's final, when France defeated the Netherlands. The come back of the female player, who won two Grand Slams in her life (Australian Open in 1995 and Roland-Garros in 2000), was thereby even more remarkable. But this victory does not rely on one person only. There is a real united team on the court and this union was to end with a success. This success makes Amelie Mauresmo so happy that she states the following: "Maybe it is due to our all-year-long selfishness that we enjoy so much those group emotions. We are lucky to practice a sport, which allows people to communicate all they have in a nice collective adventure. From my point of view, sharing is a unique experience."
Sharing victory – Victory of sharing. France defeats USA (4-1) for the first time in eleven meetings.

From left to right: Stéphanie Cohen-Aloro, Emilie Loit, Guy Forget, Mary Pierce and Amélie Mauresmo

Aged 47,

Martina Navratilova becomes the oldest participant of the Fed Cup.

2003 Davis Cup

Australian Anthem

Bad start for Spain. On Friday morning, a scandal nearly exploded when trumpeter James Morrison was playing wrong Spanish national anthem. Instead of the right anthem, he played the pre-civil war republican era one (dated before Franco). This happened in front of the Spanish team including Juan Carlos Ferrero, Carlos Moya, Alex Corretja and Feliciano Lopez, as well as their league captain Jordi Arrese. But things made worse Spanish ambassador and Spain's Secretary of State for Sports were also seated in the stadium. They both stormed from the place and left their seats empty. The players, who were also upset by this scandalous incident, protested by sitting on the court. It is a regrettable occurrence... And this is only the opening ceremony of this 2003 Davis Cup final Australia-Spain on the Australian lawn of the Rod Laver Arena in Melbourne. Upset Spanish delegation immediately demands official apology, which was to be done by John Fitzerald himself, captain of the Australian team. The game finally started. But the following events were not happier for Arrese's men. Lleyton Hewitt staged a nearly four-hour and five-set first match to upend Juan Carlos Ferrero. Nevertheless a gleam of hope appeared with 1 point taken by Carlos Moya against Mark Philippoussis. On Friday evening, competition is all square. This result could have erased the bad occurrence of the morning. But the next day, double Australian specialists Todd Woodbridge and Wayne Arthurs defeat Corretja and Lopez, which leads Australia to a score of 2-1. In spite of a shoulder injury, Mark Philippoussis gave his team the last winning point for victory. "Winning a tournament in my native town in presence of my fellow audience makes it even more wonderful", he said. Hewitt concludes as follows: "This success is even more remarkable for Australia as it is the first time in 17 years that it has been reached home by the same four guys as from the first day. This is really incredible!" Australia gets its 28th Silver Cup.

Just Too Good!

Nobody would disagree. Aged 23, Roger Federer is one level above all the others. As if he were an Alien. World No. 1 in February, he flied over the season, winning, among others, three Grand Slam titles. If he goes on with such a rhythm, he'll probably be the best player ever.

He is only 23. Some already compare him to the greatest tennis players. The greatest also admire him. Roger Federer is not a common tennis player, he is the best player on Earth for the time being, and maybe the best of all time. In any case, if he goes on like that, he will be the best ever for sure.

Since his Masters victory in 2003, Roger exhausted many players. It started with a title at the Australian Open. This victory led him to the ATP top rank (eventually). Then, he became the first Swiss man to be world No. 1, the second Swiss after Martina Hingis (in 1997, 1999 and 2000). In March, in Dubai and in the Indian Wells Masters Series, he added other victories to his list of awards. Then, the red clay court season started and he captured another Masters Series in Hamburg. In June, he excelled on grass in Halle and Wimbledon. Early July, just to show that he was not good only on fast surfaces, he won a small red clay tournament in Gstaad. One more! End of July, he managed to win a third Masters Series in Toronto. Hence, he broke another record: he was the first player since Björn Borg in 1979 to win three tournaments in a row, on three different surfaces (grass in Wimbledon, red clay in Gstaad and hard court in Toronto). At that time, he had so many points that he was already certain to take part in the Masters Cup at the end of the year (and then to be one of the eight best players of the season). As if it was not enough, in September, he captured a third Grand Slam title in Flushing Meadows. After his US Open victory, his world No. 1 rank was assured until the end of the season, even if World No. 2 (Andy Roddick) was also winning all his matches. In the beginning of October in Bangkok, he was to capture his twelfth victory in a row (this year). A record. Roger Federer is great. His winning three major titles meant that he captured a Small Slam. He is the third player to achieve this since the Open Era, after Jimmy Connors in 1974 and Mats Wilander in 1988. The Swede commented on this performance: "To win three Grand Slams is much more

difficult in 2004 than in our time." Roger Federer is so great that everybody was astonished to see his early exit from the French Open (in the third round against Gustavo Kuerten). But red clay is not really a problem for him. Roger is capable of winning everywhere. He already won on the four surfaces in 2003 and 2004 (outdoor hard court, red clay, grass, indoor hard court). This accomplishment reminds us all of Pete Sampras, the last to have reached it (in 1994). However, even tough Pete Sampras won fourteen Grand Slam titles, he never captured Roland-Garros. Just like Federer so far. "I know I can play well on red clay, the Swiss claimed. I never had any doubt about it. I already reached good results. " Indeed, Roger won twice in Hamburg (2002 in 2004), but still, he has never gone further than quarterfinals in the French Open. Would it be possible that the famous Court Central impresses him? "I would even say that the frame and the configuration of the Court Central force you to play 'small' ", he said. Just before the last French Open, he announced: "If it is not this year, it will be for another one…" It was not for this year, so it will be for another one. If he said so! And at his age, he still has many years ahead of him to capture this Parisian title. Maybe he will do better than the legendary Sampras.
The comparison with the former No.1 is flattering. At the age of 22, when he lifted his second London trophy, Roger Federer was older than Pete Sampras when he won his second Grand Slam title. However, the former waited only seven months to capture the second one, whereas the latter waited for two years and a half for a second big victory.
In Wimbledon, in 2003, John McEnroe had already named him the 'Sampras of the 21st century'. Since Federer's Australian Open victory, McEnroe said even better: "He is the most talented player I've had the pleasure to see, even more than my favourite Rod Laver and Pete Sampras. If somebody is to be chosen as the one to perform a Grand Slam, it would be him; he can defeat anybody on any surface." Another 'great' tennis player made the same comparison: "Roger evolves a bit like Pete Sampras", Agassi commented. "Pete's serve was better than his but he has a better footwork. Roger is much better behind the baseline and on a return, but his volley is not as good as Sampras's". What does he think of

> " I am surprised myself, I hope that one will not expect me to win each time. I want people to know that if I did not play my matches at 100%, I would lose half of them. "
>
> *Roger Federer*

it? "I would say I am a bit more complete than Pete Sampras. Even if my volley is not as good as his, that's just because I do not come to the net as often as he did. Otherwise both of us have a relaxed game, this is the real similarity."

Yes, Roger is very good. Players who unfortunately meet him on a court think the same. "Roger is the only player against whom I can lose a set 6/0 even if I play my top game", the French Fabrice Santoro claimed. "I think he may become the greatest player of all time, especially if he goes on progressing as he did this year", the Australian Lleyton Hewitt stated. More compliments come from Yves Allegro, one of his Davis Cup team mate: "He is like an artist, a painter or a sculptor, who gives the impression that everything is easy." And praises keep coming: "To watch Federer play is delightful to me", John McEnroe (again him!) admitted. "I would have dreamt of playing like he does. He is one of the greatest tennis champions of all time. If he goes on like that for the next three of four years, he will be the best player ever to me. He does whatever he wants on a court. He plays like every tennis player should play, using all tennis shots. He can beat you from the baseline but also easily from the net. He can play on all surfaces even if, on red clay, it is a bit harder for him. For sure he is the best, far above all the others." It would be hard to be more gratifying! The Swede Mats Wilander is less openhearted in his compliments, but as meaningful as the others. "Roger is perfect! My thanks go to him; he shows everybody that it is

possible to play tennis that way, with such perfection." The Swede was even dreaming after Federer's victory over Lleyton Hewitt in the US Open final: "I would like to be in his shoes only one day to know what he feels when he plays such a way". It is a lovely compliment, coming from a former world No. 1, who holds thirty-three titles, including seven Grand Slams.

By the way, why is Roger Federer so good? For different reasons. First of all, because Roger is quick on his feet. Andy Roddick said so: "On the court, he is not only talented but he is incredibly fast and he has an amazingly versatile game. Even from his baseline, he manages to return a shot really difficult to play." Second, because he sees better than the others. He feels the game differently. "Let's say that when I observe my opponent's technique, I generally know where he can return the ball and at which speed. It is very relevant as it shows me which part of the court I have to cover in priority. I also see where the guy will serve." Third, because he is confident: "I know what I achieved. I know what I am able to do and that is confidence." Fourth, because his progression over the last two years was impressive. Andre Agassi confirmed it: "He plays so well now! His forehand became huge, his backhand more regular, and his serve more efficient. He deserves his current rank. He is a player, who does not let you rest for a second." Fifth, because he plays all his matches at 100%: "I am surprised myself", he announced after his victory in Gstaad.

" Roger is perfect! My thanks go to him; he shows everybody that it is possible to play tennis that way, with such perfection. "

Mats Wilander

"I hope that one will not expect me to win each time. I want people to know that if I did not play my matches at 100%, I would lose half of them." Sixth, because he is hardworking. "Roger is working smartly", his fitness trainer Pierre Paganini clarified. Because Roger Federer can manage the Grand Slam's high rhythm. He does not waste all his energy in the first week. He increases his level slowly and then, pushes it as far as he can, usually until the final. At this stage of competition, the Swiss has the power. In Flushing Meadows, he was to capture his twelfth final in a row. He is the first player to win his four first Grand Slam finals. He lost only one set in the four major finals and semi-finals. Yes, we can talk about power! The least we can say is that Roger is a winner. "Since I was a junior, I always thought it was not worth playing a final to lose it. I do not want to lose in a final. I do not accept that, it is not complicated to understand."

One of his "favourite" opponents is called Andy Roddick. Seven victories (for the Swiss), for one defeat, including two victories in Wimbledon (semi-final in 2003 and final in 2004). Completely down after his defeat in the final of the Toronto Masters Series, Roddick said few words: "Congratulations Roger, but you starting to be very annoying". And Federer replied: "Sorry Andy but we will play many more finals in the future, believe me!" Roddick did not feel any resentment and he assessed his toughest opponent with all due respect: "He is obviously the best player on Earth and he deserves his world No.1", he said. "You feel a kind of aura around him, you already feel it in the locker room."

Last but not least, Roger Federer is so good because he does not like to lose. It is as simple as that. "Whatever the sport, he added. Even sport I do with my friends." When playing cards or other games, it is the same: "When I was a kid, if I lost at chess, I was so pissed off I used to throw all the pieces on the floor!" It is also to soothe this kind of behaviour that at 17 years old, he started to work hard on his mental with a psychological coach. Just to calm him down on a court. When he was younger, Roger was much more impulsive than today. "I am not the same on a court and in my life. The only similarity is that I am relaxed", he confirmed. The Federer phenomenon took some time to

become what it is. Of course, he had some huge qualities as from the beginning. Alain Rostan, the Swiss team doctor, knows about it: "He is able to manage his time. Training, friends, sponsors, private life, he gives every field the time needed. That is really impressive. And you may notice that he manages his tennis with the same care. He analyses everything." Like a computer. He is not very far from perfection.

What he can achieve without a coach proves once again that he is one level above the others. "I also think it is better to work alone than with a bad coach. However, a good coach may help a lot and I hope he won't have this additional help! He should go on like this!" Andre Agassi kidded. Indeed, it is really strange for a world No.1 not to have a coach. Reasons

> " I would have dreamt of playing like he does. He rates among the greatest tennis champions of all time. If he goes on like this for the next three of four years, he will be the best player ever to me. "
>
> *John McEnroe*

Roger is the Ninth Player to win the Small Slam

(three Grand Slam titles in one single season)

Only Rod Laver (1962, 1969) and Donald Budge (1938) achieved the grand Slam.

1	1933	**Jack Crawford** (US Open)
2	1934	**Fred Perry** (Roland-Garros)
3	1955	**Tony Trabert** (Australian Open)
4	1956	**Lewis Hoad** (US Open)
5	1958	**Ashley Cooper** (Roland-Garros)
6	1964	**Roy Emerson** (Roland-Garros)
7	1974	**Jimmy Connors** (Roland-Garros)
8	1988	**Mats Wilander** (Wimbledon)
9	2004	**Roger Federer** (Roland-Garros)

(Between brackets the Grand Slam title they were missing that year).

Roger FEDERER

(Statistics dated from November 1, 2004)

Birth date: August 8, 1981
Birthplace: Basel, Switzerland
Height: 6'1"
Weight: 177 lbs.
Best ranking: No. 1 (February 2, 2004)
List of awards: 21 titles

2004	Australian Open, Dubai, TMS Indian Wells, TMS Hamburg, Halle, Wimbledon, Gstaad, TMS Toronto, US Open, Bangkok.
2003	Marseille, Dubai, Munich, Halle, Wimbledon, Vienne, Masters Cup.
2002	Sydney, TMS Hamburg, Vienna.
2001	Milan.

for this belong to human relationship only. For the time being, he does not need a coach. At least he wants to have relationship based on trust, a perfect osmosis with such a person: "For me, the coach also has to be a friend. We share our lives. We spend the whole season together. What is sure is that I could not go and have lunch with someboby with whom I do not have a friendly relationship." However, the cooperation with his previous coach Peter Lundgren had been good. But apparently it was enough for the time being. "Moreover, I talk a lot with the journalists. Expressing things helps me have a better understanding. Before, when I was at a press conference, I told them more than my coach!" he explained. Federer thinks each player should know himself what he needs. He does not have a coach but he has a whole team taking care of him; a physiotherapist (Pavel Kovac) and a fitness coach (Pierre Paganini). To him, the latter is necessary to face the harsh rhythm of the season. He also chose Miroslava Vavrinec, his girlfriend since 2000, to take care of his relations with the press. "He knows what he's doing, Marc Rosset, Swiss national coach, said. He is well organised, all is going well with the people around him. And Mirka (Miroslava) had a key role in his life: thanks to her, he grew up very quickly, he became a man. Former Roger,

who used to play Playstation for hours and throw his rackets on the floor during training, is now a great pro." And Federer added: "I do not see why I should change my habits. For the time being it seems to work rather well." Indeed, why change a winning formula?

Therefore, with so many qualities, how is it possible to beat him? As per Mats Wilander, there may be one solution: "You can not beat Roger trying to be better than him. It is impossible. But you can beat him by doing utmost to crush him. Then he will maybe start worrying. It is the only possibility to face his perfection." Heard ? But Arnaud Clement does not agree: "As 'Scud' (Nicolas Escude) told me, Roger is like the wizard Harry Potter, so to beat him, you just have to steal his witch broom from him!" So nobody really knows the solution, except to cut one of his legs or hands…But even so…

The most perfect? Almost. He was thought to be indestructible but at the end of October, the Swiss was injured before the Basel tournament - a thigh laceration. Would he also belong to the human race? Roger Brennwald, the tournament's manager, had stated when he heard the news: "We work with human beings, not with machines." This time it has been clearly said.

One, Two...and Three!

A third 100% Belgian final match in a Grand Slam tournament. World No. 1 Justine Henin-Hardenne once again beats Kim Clijsters and captures her third Grand Slam title in her career. Even though she was injured after having reached the fourth round, the French tennis player, Amelie Mauresmo, becomes World No. 3.

" Two years ago, or twelve
months ago, I couldn't have won
this kind of match, that's for sure.
Today, I did. So that's great
progress. "

Justine Henin-Hardenne

" I felt I played well today;
I played as I had never played in
the last finals against Justine. "

Kim Clijsters

Justine Henin-Hardenne

Justine Henin-Hardenne started off the year very
well. She won a title in Sydney (Tier II, US$
585,000), and then a third Grand Slam title at the
Australian Open. Out of the four last Grand Slams'
finals, she captured three titles (Roland-Garros and
US Open in 2003, Melbourne in 2004) and lost
only one (against Venus Williams in Wimbledon in
2001). In all three Grand Slam victories, she played
countrywoman Kim Clijsters. 21-years-old Justine
arrived in Melbourne in the shoes of a World No. 1
tennis player. It was the first time in her career that
she was starting a Grand Slam tournament as top-
seed. Therefore, she had to deal with a lot of
pressure. For the third time in eight months, the
two Belgian girls met in such an important final
match. Lleyton Hewitt's fiancée, logically supported
by the Australian audience, didn't give in during
the whole match. Despite Justine's 6/3, 4/2 lead,
Kim won the next four games, took the set and
levelled the match at one set all. "I was feeling very
anxious to finish the match", Henin-Hardenne
admitted later. Clijsters saw Henin-Hardenne break
her twice in the third set and was quickly led 4-0.
"At this time of the match, I thought I just had to
make her play. And then she made some faults
when coming to the net. I just had to go on
fighting." Clijsters explained later. That's how the
Flemish player managed to break her compatriot's
next 2 serves. "I was feeling Kim was very strong
mentally. At the end, the fight was very tight."
World No. 1 admitted later. But Clijsters's revival
happened too late to give some kind of worry to
the Walloon girl. Justine defeated Kim 6/3, 4/6, 6/3
in 1.47 hour.
Kim's disappointment was strong: "I felt I was
playing today like I had never played in the last
finals against Justine." Her disappointment was
even greater because if she had earned this first

Grand Slam title, she would have had taken back her World No. 1 rank from Justine, which logically remained hers after this tournament.

"To reach the final match here means more to me than at Roland-Garros or at the US Open. I feel very well and I have crowd's support." Kim Clijsters said after her semi-final match. The 20-year-old girl reached four finals in Grand Slams tournaments without winning any. Previous World No. 1 still needs to win a big title. She sadly equals record of Venus Williams and Martina Hingis. As for Justine, she is

3 Only three girls out of 128 attending the Australian Open 2004 had captured at least one Grand Slam title before: Venus Williams, Lindsay Davenport (the only one who already won in Melbourne) and Justine Henin-Hardenne.

Sydney's Revelation

She turned 16 on January 25.

The revelation of this Open is called Tatiana Golovin. She is French. She received an invitation for the first round of the Australian Open thanks to an agreement between Australian and French federations. She beat top seeds No. 14 Anna Smashnova-Pistolesi and No. 23 Lina Krasnoroutskaya, and didn't lose one single set. To celebrate her 16th birthday on January 25, she won the third round and advanced to the fourth. Not too bad, for a 16-year-old girl! As a result of her great play, she became the youngest French to go that far in such a Grand Slam competition. The American Lisa Raymond sharply awoke her from her dream defeating her in the fourth round (6/2, 6/0). "It is not the best way to leave a tournament but I will keep this wonderful week in my memory forever." The Russian girl, who left her home country to improve her tennis at Nick Bollettieri academy when she was seven and a half, was ranked 354 before the Australian Open. Her achievement there allowed her to leap over 218 ranks and reach the 136th.

Tatiana Golovin

missing only one Grand Slam title to have them all, that of Wimbledon.

Several top players couldn't make it to the first Grand Slam of the 2004 season. In addition to defending title-holder, Serena Williams, other former winners of the tournament had to pull out: Jennifer Capriati (winner in 2001 and 2002), Mary Pierce (in 1995), Monica Seles (from 1991 to 1993 and in 1996). Serena Williams still suffering from her left knee, Seles from her left foot, Capriati from her back; and Pierce is not prepared well enough.
Amelie Mauresmo had to give up on a good draw that might have had her play Justine Henin-Hardenne in the semi-finals and possibly reach the final. The Frenchwoman had reached the quarter-finals but had to withdraw due to a left mid-back muscle strain. The day before her match against Fabiola Zuluaga, she wanted to go to practice. She just had to check whether

Kim and Justine

Amelie Mauresmo bursts into tears during a press conference.

her body had been playing a bad joke on her or not. At a press conference a few hours later, Amelie, tearful, made official her leave from the tournament. She was very disappointed, especially because she had brightly started, losing only six games in 3 matches. Only Australian Alicia Molik stood up to her in the fourth round (7/5, 7/5). Was it the match she shouldn't have played? "I do remember very well the exact moment I hurt myself: while stretching for a backhand volley. I felt a strong pain in my back. I was able to finish the match because my muscle was still warm. I am very frustrated to leave this cheerful tournament without even going on the court", she comments. For a consolation, the French No. 1 left Melbourne World No. 3 (on Feb. 02). It was her best rank so far. Thanks to Mauresmo's withdrawal, Fabiola Zuluaga is the first Colombian woman to reach the quarterfinals at a Grand Slam. Unfortunately for her, she was defeated 6/2 - 6/2 by the champion to be.
In some way injuries turned out to be the stars of the tournament. The hard rhythm of the seasons for sure played a role in girls' injuries and tiredness.

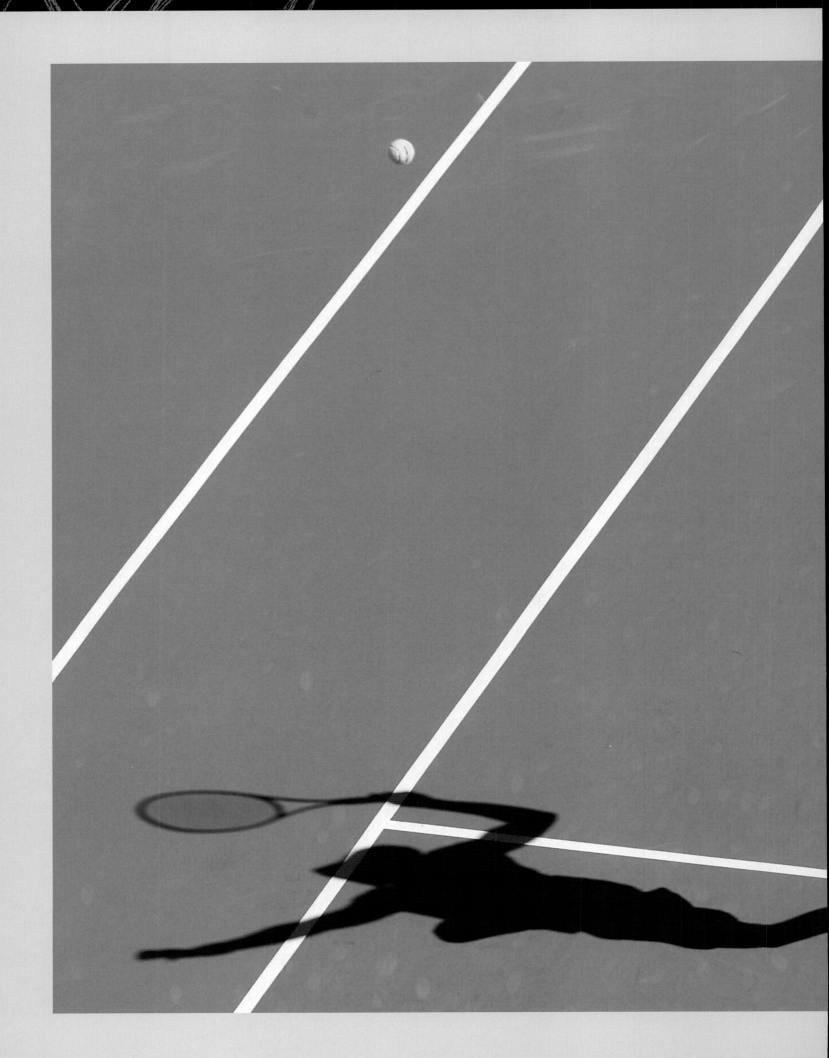

Great Start for Federer

Federer started this year at the Australian Open playing an aggressive game. Not only did he defeat the amazing Russian Marat Safin, but he also took the lead in the world ranking (at last). And this was only a start.

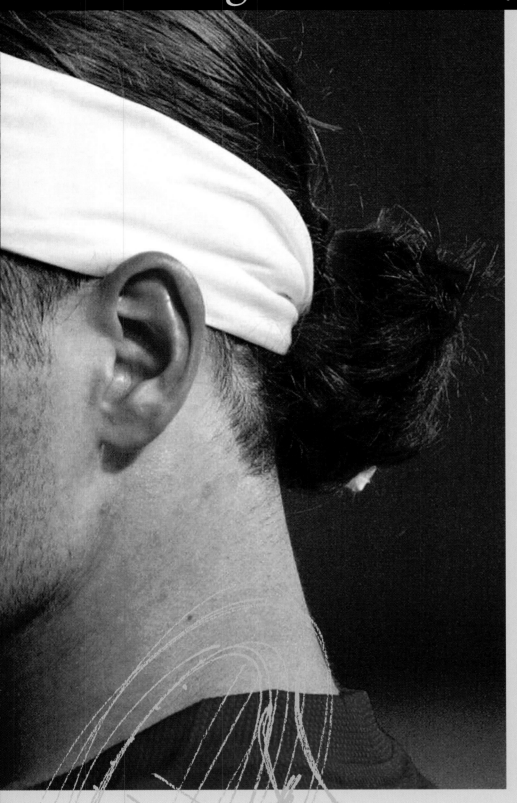

We can consider it as a warning: Roger Federer wasn't going to stand aside this year. We would have to get used to his winning Grand Slam titles and to his being world No. 1, where he belongs. This is at least what his Australian performance let us believe. Federer's victory against Juan Carlos Ferrero (seeded 3rd) in the semi-finals (6/4, 6/1, 6/4 in 1.30 hour) enabled him (ranked 2nd) to take the lead of the World Ranking, replacing Andy Roddick. "There is a lot of joy, satisfaction and pride in becoming the first Swiss to make it to No. 1 (on the men's side). Sometimes I may have a poker face, but I was really nervous knowing this could happen tonight."

He was self-confident at the beginning of the final against the former world No. 1, Marat Safin. The Swiss was strengthened with experience and took advantage of his 78 victories in 2003, his 7 titles, including Wimbledon (his first Grand Slam), and his Masters victory two months earlier.

The Swiss had dropped only two sets throughout the tournament (one against Lleyton Hewitt and another one against David Nalbandian).

As for the Russian, he had lost nine sets and had played three five-set matches. Therefore Safin didn't only have to fight the Swiss but also his fatigue.

Just like in the Wimbledon final match against Mark Philippoussis, it took Federer only 3 straight sets to stop giant-killing run of the Russian Marat Safin. Safin served 33 aces against Agassi but Federer was unable to return only three serves, broke Safin five times in 15 serves, and ended up winning 7/6 (3), 6/4, 6/2.

"I knew Marat has the proper game to win this tournament, but I didn't think he would have got it back so quickly after such a long absence. We are all glad to see him back but also a bit worried about it. Marat is one of the

> " There is only one time you get to No. 1 for the first time in your career. I really want to enjoy it. "
>
> *Roger Federer*

> " I never would have thought of reaching the final, after what happened to me last year. I had to start all over again. "
>
> *Marat Safin*

Marat Safin

best on this surface", the Swiss commented after the final.

Apart from that, the players who shone like stars in 2003 failed to confirm their status this year. The unexpected finalist of the previous Australian Open, Rainer Schuettler, was defeated by the young fiery Swedish Robin Soderling. The German was weakened by the extra hours he played during last November's Masters. Carlos Moya (world No. 7), Younes El Aynaoui, Nicolas Massu, Mardy Fish, Arnaud Clement, Vince Spadea and Tommy Robredo were also defeated; that makes a total of eight top seeds out of the competition as from the first day. On women's side, six names disappeared straight away from the list of top players for this tournament (Serna, Shaughnessy, Pisnik, Petrova, Dementieva and Tanasugarn).

For the first time since 1993, the four semi-finalists had earned at least one Grand Slam title. Andre Agassi, Marat Safin, Roger Federer and Juan Carlos Ferrero took the place of Pete Sampras, Jim Courier, Michael Stich and Stefan Edberg, all semi-finalists in 1993.

The Spaniard Juan Carlos Ferrero had good reasons to be frustrated. If he had not lost the match against Federer, he would have had a chance to recover his world No. 1 rank since Andy Roddick lost the semi-finals against Safin.

Hicham Arazi

Weakened by constant pain in a nagging leg, Ferrero admitted he was impatient to play this semi-final match against the Swiss: "I think that if I am 100 percent, I could win the match", he claims after defeat. "I've been playing so well for the last two weeks! But today, I was not so good. I could get the ball only 3 or 4 times consecutively!" The Spaniard had already felt some pain in his leg when he was playing his second match against Filippo Volandri. Pain got sharper during the next round against Andrei Pavel. "I was taking anti-inflammatory pills but it wasn't enough to be okay" Ferrero said. "I am a bit disappointed. Semi-finals at the Australian Open is not so bad but I am convinced I could have gone further!" Ferrero may be convinced of whatever he wants, in the end Federer did win. He is considered as the most complete player in tennis history. He is capable of winning the four Grand Slams. At age 22, he is already half way through.

Juan Carlos Ferrero

Andre Agassi

The match

Quarterfinals. Safin won over Roddick 2/6, 6/3, 7/5, 6/7, 6/4.

World No. 1 Andy Roddick is considered as the top favourite for quarterfinals against the Russian Marat Safin, ranked 86th before the tournament. The American didn't drop any set over the last two weeks. Safin spent much more time on the court (11.43 hours, against 5.50 for Roddick) beating among others Jarkko Nieminen, Todd Martin and James Blake. The first set was a piece of cake for the American. But Safin managed to come back in the second set, putting Roddick off his baseline game. Safin, who had stated that he wanted to reach world No. 1 by the end of the season, defeated the American after 3.23 hours of fierce struggle. Marat Safin advanced to the semi-finals of a grand Slam for the first time since Roland-Garros in 2002. "I am back", he said at the end of the match. A wrist injury had put him out of competition for one year. Due to his defeat, Andy Roddick lost his No. 1 ranking, which was taken by Roger Federer. "I think I played well tonight", he said. "We always learn more through defeats than victories." Safin won't forget this victory also because he was celebrating his twenty fourth birthday: "I can't ask for anything else. It's probably the best birthday I ever had, especially with 15,000 people singing."

44

44 minutes is the time Sebastien Grosjean (seed No. 10) resisted Andre Agassi. He gave up in the quarterfinals against the American when he was led 6/2, 2/0, due to a groin pain. "I now know this kind of pain, better not to insist" he thinks. Diagnosis after coming back to France: three weeks of full rest due to groin strain.

AUSTRALIAN OPEN

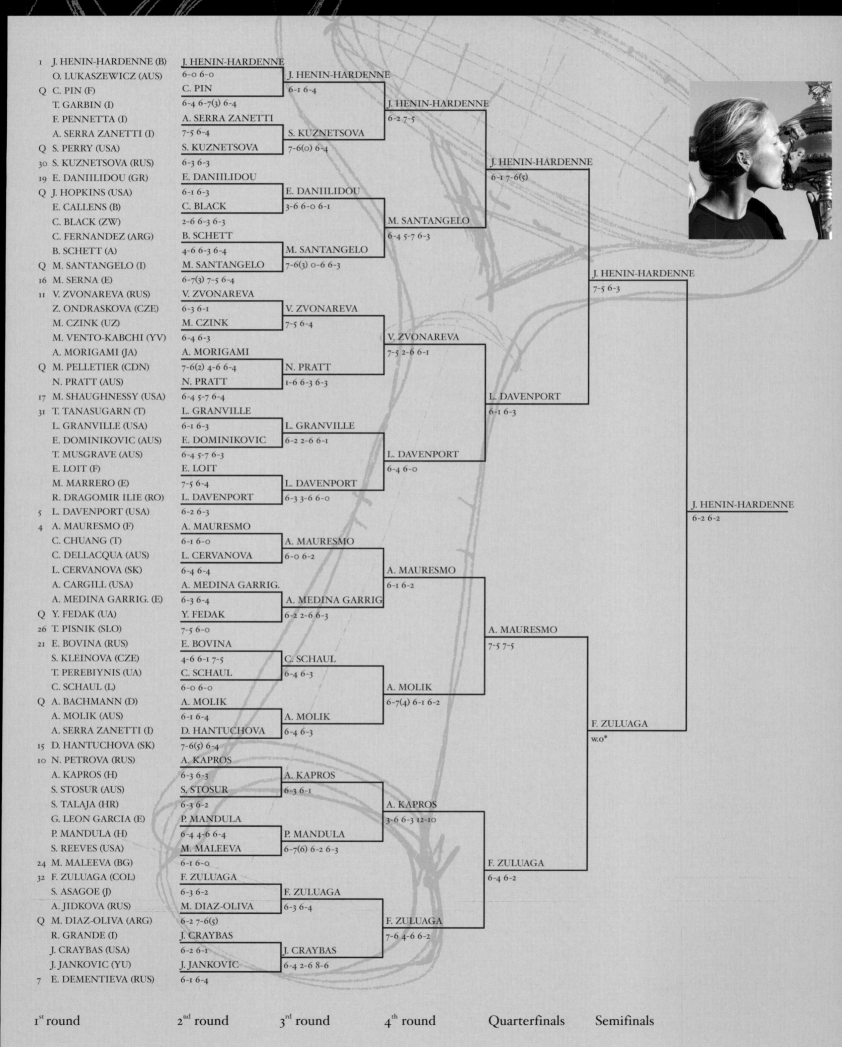

| 1st round | 2nd round | 3rd round | 4th round | Quarterfinals | Semifinals |

1 J. HENIN-HARDENNE (B)
O. LUKASZEWICZ (AUS)
Q C. PIN (F)
T. GARBIN (I)
F. PENNETTA (I)
A. SERRA ZANETTI (I)
Q S. PERRY (USA)
30 S. KUZNETSOVA (RUS)
19 E. DANIILIDOU (GR)
Q J. HOPKINS (USA)
E. CALLENS (B)
C. BLACK (ZW)
C. FERNANDEZ (ARG)
B. SCHETT (A)
Q M. SANTANGELO (I)
16 M. SERNA (E)
11 V. ZVONAREVA (RUS)
Z. ONDRASKOVA (CZE)
M. CZINK (UZ)
M. VENTO-KABCHI (YV)
A. MORIGAMI (JA)
Q M. PELLETIER (CDN)
N. PRATT (AUS)
17 M. SHAUGHNESSY (USA)
31 T. TANASUGARN (T)
L. GRANVILLE (USA)
E. DOMINIKOVIC (AUS)
T. MUSGRAVE (AUS)
E. LOIT (F)
M. MARRERO (E)
R. DRAGOMIR ILIE (RO)
5 L. DAVENPORT (USA)
4 A. MAURESMO (F)
C. CHUANG (T)
C. DELLACQUA (AUS)
L. CERVANOVA (SK)
A. CARGILL (USA)
A. MEDINA GARRIG. (E)
Q Y. FEDAK (UA)
26 T. PISNIK (SLO)
21 E. BOVINA (RUS)
S. KLEINOVA (CZE)
T. PEREBIYNIS (UA)
C. SCHAUL (L)
Q A. BACHMANN (D)
A. MOLIK (AUS)
A. SERRA ZANETTI (I)
15 D. HANTUCHOVA (SK)
10 N. PETROVA (RUS)
A. KAPROS (H)
S. STOSUR (AUS)
S. TALAJA (HR)
G. LEON GARCIA (E)
P. MANDULA (H)
S. REEVES (USA)
24 M. MALEEVA (BG)
32 F. ZULUAGA (COL)
S. ASAGOE (J)
A. JIDKOVA (RUS)
Q M. DIAZ-OLIVA (ARG)
R. GRANDE (I)
J. CRAYBAS (USA)
J. JANKOVIC (YU)
7 E. DEMENTIEVA (RUS)

J. HENIN-HARDENNE 6-0 6-0
C. PIN 6-4 6-7(3) 6-4
A. SERRA ZANETTI 7-5 6-4
S. KUZNETSOVA 6-3 6-3
E. DANIILIDOU 6-1 6-3
C. BLACK 2-6 6-3 6-3
B. SCHETT 4-6 6-3 6-4
M. SANTANGELO 7-6(3) 0-6 6-3
V. ZVONAREVA 6-3 6-1
M. CZINK 6-4 6-3
A. MORIGAMI 7-6(2) 4-6 6-4
N. PRATT 1-6 6-3 6-3
L. GRANVILLE 6-1 6-3
E. DOMINIKOVIC 6-4 5-7 6-3
E. LOIT 7-5 6-4
L. DAVENPORT 6-3 3-6 6-0
A. MAURESMO 6-1 6-0
L. CERVANOVA 6-4 6-4
A. MEDINA GARRIG. 6-3 6-4
Y. FEDAK 7-5 6-0
E. BOVINA 4-6 6-1 7-5
C. SCHAUL 6-0 6-0
A. MOLIK 6-1 6-4
D. HANTUCHOVA 7-6(5) 6-4
A. KAPROS 6-3 6-3
S. STOSUR 6-3 6-2
P. MANDULA 6-4 4-6 6-4
M. MALEEVA 6-1 6-0
F. ZULUAGA 6-3 6-2
M. DIAZ-OLIVA 6-2 7-6(5)
J. CRAYBAS 6-2 6-1
J. JANKOVIC 6-1 6-4

J. HENIN-HARDENNE 6-1 6-4
S. KUZNETSOVA 7-6(0) 6-4
E. DANIILIDOU 3-6 6-0 6-1
M. SANTANGELO 6-4 5-7 6-3
V. ZVONAREVA 7-5 6-4
N. PRATT 6-4 5-7 6-4
L. GRANVILLE 6-2 2-6 6-1
L. DAVENPORT 6-4 6-0
A. MAURESMO 6-0 6-2
A. MEDINA GARRIG 6-2 2-6 6-3
C. SCHAUL 6-4 6-3
A. MOLIK 6-4 6-3
A. KAPROS 6-3 6-1
P. MANDULA 6-7(6) 6-2 6-3
F. ZULUAGA 6-3 6-4
J. CRAYBAS 6-4 2-6 8-6

J. HENIN-HARDENNE 6-2 7-5
M. SANTANGELO 6-4 5-7 6-3
V. ZVONAREVA 7-5 2-6 6-1
L. DAVENPORT 6-4 6-0
A. MAURESMO 6-1 6-2
A. MOLIK 6-7(4) 6-1 6-2
A. KAPROS 3-6 6-3 12-10
F. ZULUAGA 7-6 4-6 6-2

J. HENIN-HARDENNE 6-1 7-6(5)
L. DAVENPORT 6-1 6-3
A. MAURESMO 7-5 7-5
F. ZULUAGA 6-4 6-2

J. HENIN-HARDENNE 7-5 6-3
F. ZULUAGA w.o*

J. HENIN-HARDENNE 6-2 6-2

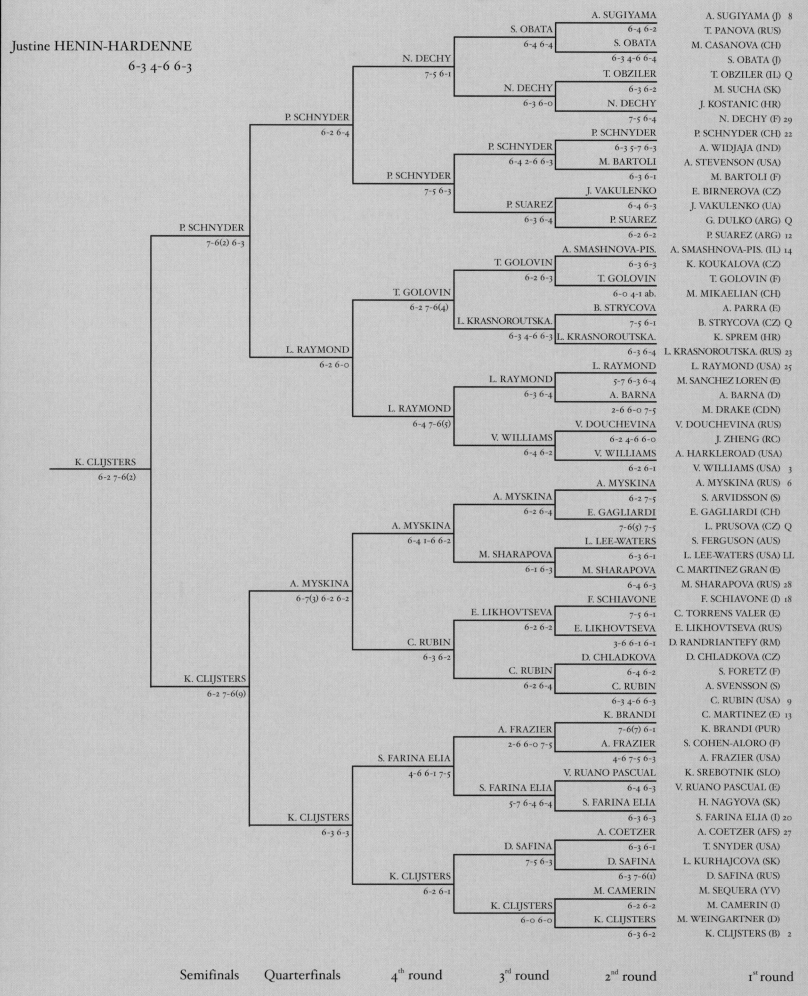

Justine HENIN-HARDENNE
6-3 4-6 6-3

| Semifinals | Quarterfinals | 4th round | 3rd round | 2nd round | 1st round |

AUSTRALIAN OPEN

| 1st round | 2nd round | 3rd round | 4th round | Quarterfinals | Semifinals |

1st round

1 A. RODDICK (USA)
F. GONZALEZ (RCH)
B. ULIHRACH (CZ)
L. BURGSMULLER (D)
I. LABADZE (GE)
J. CHELA (ARG)
F. VERDASCO (E)
27 T. DENT (USA)
18 Y. EL AYNAOUI (MA)
G. BLANCO (E)
J. MELZER (A)
T. BEHREND (D)
D. FERRER (E)
Q G. MULLER (L)
Q K. CARLSEN (DK)
16 S. SCHALKEN (NL)
12 N. MASSU (RCH)
J. NIEMINEN (FIN)
M. SAFIN (RUS)
B. VAHALY (USA)
A. DUPUIS (F)
T. MARTIN (USA)
I. KARLOVIC (HR)
21 M. FISH (USA)
30 A. CLEMENT (F)
N. DAVYDENKO (RUS)
Q O. PATIENCE (F)
I. ANDREEV (RUS)
O. HERNANDEZ (E)
N. LAPENTTI (EC)
J. BLAKE (USA)
I. MIRANDA (PE)
4 A. AGASSI (USA)
T. LARKHAM (AUS)
N. MAHUT (F)
Q T. BERDYCH (CZ)
K. BECK (SK)
S. KOUBEK (AUT)
T. ENQVIST (S)
29 V. SPADEA (USA)
19 G. KUERTEN (BR)
J. VAN LOTTUM (NL)
D. TURSUNOV (RUS)
I. LJUBICIC (HR)
Q J. GOLMARD (F)
A. PORTAS (E)
J. ACASUSO (ARG)
13 P. SRICHAPHAN (T)
9 S. GROSJEAN (F)
M. YOUZHNY (RUS)
J. GAMBILL (USA)
G. CARRAZ (F)
D. HRBATY (SK)
F. SARETTA (BR)
G. GAUDIO (ARG)
20 T. ROBREDO (E)
32 R. GINEPRI (USA)
L. HORNA (PE)
C. GUCCIONE (AUS)
A. JONES (AUS)
N. ESCUDE (F)
H. LEE (KOR)
R. SODERLING (S)
6 R. SCHUETTLER (D)

2nd round

A. RODDICK
6-2 7-5 7-6(4)
B. ULIHRACH
6-4 3-6 6-2 6-1
J. CHELA
6-4 6-3 3-6 6-3
T. DENT
6-2 6-1 2-1 ab.
G. BLANCO
4-1 ab.
J. MELZER
6-1 6-2 6-2
D. FERRER
7-6(4) 6-1 6-3
S. SCHALKEN
7-5 6-3 6-1
J. NIEMINEN
6-1 6-7(5) 6-2 6-3
M. SAFIN
6-2 3-6 6-3 6-4
T. MARTIN
4-6 4-6 7-6(5) 7-6(4) 6-3
I. KARLOVIC
7-6(0) 7-6(5) 7-6(4)
N. DAVYDENKO
6-7(6) 4-6 6-4 6-1 6-2
O. PATIENCE
4-6 4-6 7-6(4) 6-1 6-2
N. LAPENTTI
6-1 6-3 6-1
J. BLAKE
6-1 6-4 6-4
A. AGASSI
6-1 6-3 6-4
T. BERDYCH
6-4 6-2 5-7 6-3
K. BECK
6-4 6-0 2-6 6-4
T. ENQVIST
4-6 6-4 6-4 7-6(6)
G. KUERTEN
5-7 6-0 6-1 2-6 8-6
I. LJUBICIC
7-6(2) 6-4 5-7 6-2
J. GOLMARD
7-6(3) 6-4 6-1
P. SRICHAPHAN
7-5 6-4 6-0
S. GROSJEAN
6-1 6-4 7-5
J. GAMBILL
6-2 6-3 ab.
D. HRBATY
6-3 6-3 6-3
G. GAUDIO
6-3 6-2 7-6(6)
R. GINEPRI
7-5 6-3 6-3
C. GUCCIONE
6-3 7-6(3) 6-2
N. ESCUDE
6-3 7-6(5) 6-2
R. SODERLING
4-6 4-6 7-5 6-3 6-4

3rd round

A. RODDICK
6-2 6-2 6-3
T. DENT
3-6 6-4 4-6 7-6(4) 7-5
J. MELZER
6-3 6-4 6-3
S. SCHALKEN
6-3 6-2 5-7 6-1
M. SAFIN
7-6(5) 6-4 4-6 6-4
T. MARTIN
7-6(4) 7-6(4) 7-6(7)
O. PATIENCE
7-6(2) 6-7(7) 6-3 6-2
J. BLAKE
6-3 7-6(4) 2-6 6-1
A. AGASSI
6-0 6-2 6-4
T. ENQVIST
7-5 4-6 6-3 6-4
G. KUERTEN
7-5 6-7(5) 6-4 6-3
P. SRICHAPHAN
6-3 ab.
S. GROSJEAN
6-4 6-3 6-2
D. HRBATY
6-1 7-5 6-0
R. GINEPRI
6-4 6-3 6-3
N. ESCUDE
6-3 7-6(4) 6-4

4th round

A. RODDICK
6-2 6-0 6-2
S. SCHALKEN
7-6(1) 6-4 6-1
M. SAFIN
5-7 1-6 6-4 6-0 7-5
J. BLAKE
6-1 6-3 6-2
A. AGASSI
6-0 6-3 6-3
P. SRICHAPHAN
6-3 7-5 6-4
S. GROSJEAN
2-6 6-4 6-1 6-3
R. GINEPRI
6-2 6-3 6-4

Quarterfinals

A. RODDICK
6-1 6-2 6-3
M. SAFIN
7-6(3) 6-3 6-7(6) 6-3
A. AGASSI
7-6(3) 6-3 6-4
S. GROSJEAN
6-4 3-6 6-4 6-1

Semifinals

M. SAFIN
2-6 6-3 7-5 6-7(0) 6-4
A. AGASSI
6-2 2-0 w.o*

M. SAFIN
7-6(6) 7-6(6) 5-7 1-6 6-3

Roger FEDERER

7-6(3) 6-4 6-2

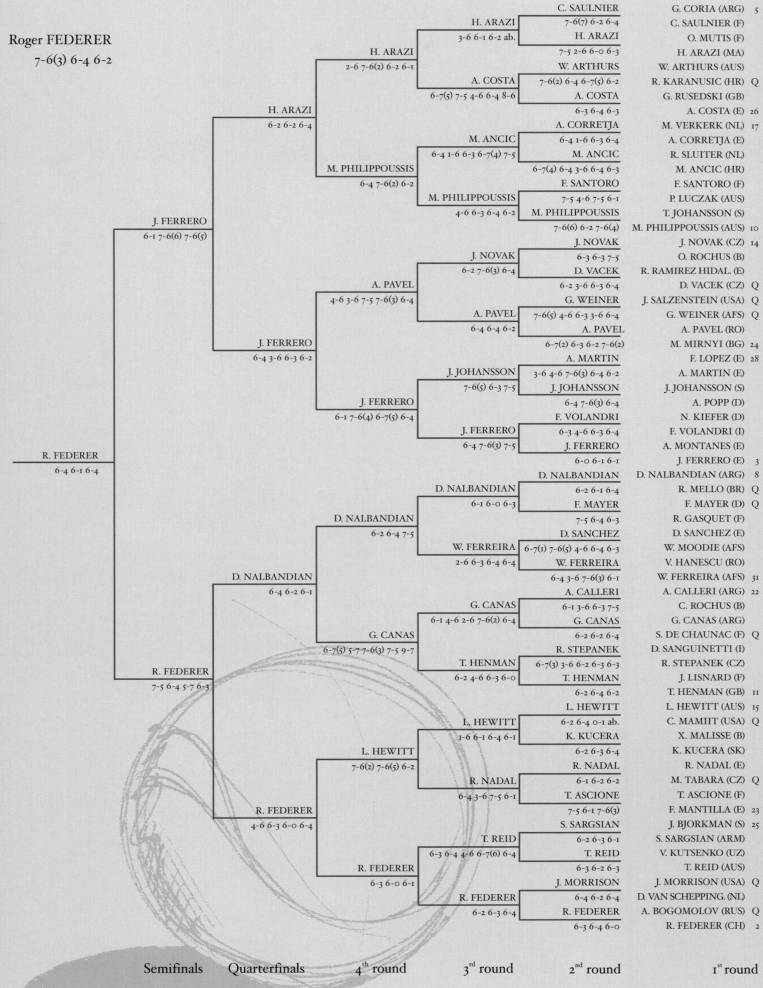

						C. SAULNIER		G. CORIA (ARG)	5
					H. ARAZI	7-6(7) 6-2 6-4		C. SAULNIER (F)	
					3-6 6-1 6-2 ab.	H. ARAZI		O. MUTIS (F)	
				H. ARAZI		7-5 2-6 6-0 6-3		H. ARAZI (MA)	
				2-6 7-6(2) 6-2 6-1		W. ARTHURS		W. ARTHURS (AUS)	
					A. COSTA	7-6(2) 6-4 6-7(5) 6-2		R. KARANUSIC (HR)	Q
					6-7(5) 7-5 4-6 6-4 8-6	A. COSTA		G. RUSEDSKI (GB)	
		H. ARAZI				6-3 6-4 6-3		A. COSTA (E)	26
		6-2 6-2 6-4				A. CORRETJA		M. VERKERK (NL)	17
					M. ANCIC	6-4 1-6 6-3 6-4		A. CORRETJA (E)	
					6-4 1-6 6-3 6-7(4) 7-5	M. ANCIC		R. SLUITER (NL)	
				M. PHILIPPOUSSIS		6-7(4) 6-4 3-6 6-4 6-3		M. ANCIC (HR)	
				6-4 7-6(2) 6-2		F. SANTORO		F. SANTORO (F)	
					M. PHILIPPOUSSIS	7-5 4-6 7-5 6-1		P. LUCZAK (AUS)	
					4-6 6-3 6-4 6-2	M. PHILIPPOUSSIS		T. JOHANSSON (S)	
	J. FERRERO					7-6(6) 6-2 7-6(4)		M. PHILIPPOUSSIS (AUS)	10
	6-1 7-6(6) 7-6(5)					J. NOVAK		J. NOVAK (CZ)	14
					J. NOVAK	6-3 6-3 7-5		O. ROCHUS (B)	
					6-2 7-6(3) 6-4	D. VACEK		R. RAMIREZ HIDAL. (E)	
				A. PAVEL		6-2 3-6 6-3 6-4		D. VACEK (CZ)	Q
				4-6 3-6 7-5 7-6(3) 6-4		G. WEINER		J. SALZENSTEIN (USA)	Q
					A. PAVEL	7-6(5) 4-6 6-3 3-6 6-4		G. WEINER (AFS)	Q
					6-4 6-4 6-2	A. PAVEL		A. PAVEL (RO)	
		J. FERRERO				6-7(2) 6-3 6-2 7-6(2)		M. MIRNYI (BG)	24
		6-4 3-6 6-3 6-2				A. MARTIN		F. LOPEZ (E)	28
					J. JOHANSSON	3-6 4-6 7-6(3) 6-4 6-2		A. MARTIN (E)	
					7-6(5) 6-3 7-5	J. JOHANSSON		J. JOHANSSON (S)	
				J. FERRERO		6-4 7-6(3) 6-4		A. POPP (D)	
				6-1 7-6(4) 6-7(5) 6-4		F. VOLANDRI		N. KIEFER (D)	
					J. FERRERO	6-3 4-6 6-3 6-4		F. VOLANDRI (I)	
					6-4 7-6(3) 7-5	J. FERRERO		A. MONTANES (E)	
R. FEDERER						6-0 6-1 6-1		J. FERRERO (E)	3
6-4 6-1 6-4						D. NALBANDIAN		D. NALBANDIAN (ARG)	8
					D. NALBANDIAN	6-2 6-1 6-4		R. MELLO (BR)	Q
					6-1 6-0 6-3	F. MAYER		F. MAYER (D)	Q
				D. NALBANDIAN		7-5 6-4 6-3		R. GASQUET (F)	
				6-2 6-4 7-5		D. SANCHEZ		D. SANCHEZ (E)	
					W. FERREIRA	6-7(1) 7-6(5) 4-6 6-4 6-3		W. MOODIE (AFS)	
					2-6 6-3 6-4 6-4	W. FERREIRA		V. HANESCU (RO)	
		D. NALBANDIAN				6-4 3-6 7-6(3) 6-1		W. FERREIRA (AFS)	31
		6-4 6-2 6-1				A. CALLERI		A. CALLERI (ARG)	22
					G. CANAS	6-1 3-6 6-3 7-5		C. ROCHUS (B)	
					6-1 4-6 2-6 7-6(2) 6-4	G. CANAS		G. CANAS (ARG)	
				G. CANAS		6-2 6-2 6-4		S. DE CHAUNAC (F)	Q
				6-7(5) 5-7 7-6(3) 7-5 9-7		R. STEPANEK		D. SANGUINETTI (I)	
					T. HENMAN	6-7(3) 3-6 6-2 6-3 6-3		R. STEPANEK (CZ)	
					6-2 4-6 6-3 6-0	T. HENMAN		J. LISNARD (F)	
	R. FEDERER					6-2 6-4 6-2		T. HENMAN (GB)	11
	7-5 6-4 5-7 6-3					L. HEWITT		L. HEWITT (AUS)	15
					L. HEWITT	6-2 6-4 0-1 ab.		C. MAMIIT (USA)	Q
					1-6 6-1 6-4 6-1	K. KUCERA		X. MALISSE (B)	
				L. HEWITT		6-2 6-3 6-4		K. KUCERA (SK)	
				7-6(2) 7-6(5) 6-2		R. NADAL		R. NADAL (E)	
					R. NADAL	6-1 6-2 6-2		M. TABARA (CZ)	Q
					6-4 3-6 7-5 6-1	T. ASCIONE		T. ASCIONE (F)	
		R. FEDERER				7-5 6-1 7-6(3)		F. MANTILLA (E)	23
		4-6 6-3 6-0 6-4				S. SARGSIAN		J. BJORKMAN (S)	25
					T. REID	6-2 6-3 6-1		S. SARGSIAN (ARM)	
					6-3 6-4 4-6 6-7(6) 6-4	T. REID		V. KUTSENKO (UZ)	
				R. FEDERER		6-3 6-2 6-3		T. REID (AUS)	
				6-3 6-0 6-1		J. MORRISON		J. MORRISON (USA)	Q
					R. FEDERER	6-4 6-2 6-4		D. VAN SCHEPPING. (NL)	
					6-2 6-3 6-4	R. FEDERER		A. BOGOMOLOV (RUS)	Q
						6-3 6-4 6-0		R. FEDERER (CH)	2

Semifinals   Quarterfinals   4th round   3rd round   2nd round   1st round

*walkover

The finalists (statistics dated February 02, 2004)

Justine Henin-Hardenne

Belgium
Birthdate: June 1, 1982
Birthplace: Marloie, Belgium
Height: 5'5 3/4"
Weight: 126 lbs.
Plays: Right-handed
Pro since: 1999
Best WTA ranking: No. 1 (October 20, 2003)
List of awards: 19 singles titles, including 3 Grand Slams (Roland-Garros 2003, US Open 2003 and Australian Open 2004)

Kim Clijsters

Belgium
Birthdate: August 8, 1983
Birthplace: Bilzen, Belgium
Height: 5'8 1/2"
Weight: 150 lbs.
Plays: Right-handed
Pro since: 1999
Best WTA ranking: No. 1(for the 1st time on August 18, 2003).
Awards: 19 titles (no Grand Slam)

Roger Federer

Switzerland
Birthdate: August 8, 1981
Birthplace: Basel, Switzerland
Height: 6'1"
Weight: 177 lbs.
Plays: Right-handed
Pro since: 1998
Best ranking: No. 1 (February 2, 2004)
List of awards: 12 titles, including 2 Grand Slams (Wimbledon 2003 and Australian Open 2004)

Marat Safin

Russia
Birthdate: January 27, 1980
Birthplace: Moscow, Russia
Height: 6'4"
Weight: 195 lbs.
Plays: Right-handed
Pro since: 1997
Best ranking: No. 1 (November 20, 2000)
List of awards: 11 titles, including 1 Grand Slam (US Open 2000)

Junior girls

Singles-Doubles

16-year-old Israeli Shahar Peer is the new Open Junior champion. Seeded No. 13, she had to face some difficulties before winning the title. At the second round, she frightened herself while playing Australian Sophie Ferguson (3/6, 6/1, 6/1). In semi-finals she defeated seeded No. 14 Swiss Timea Bacsinszky (7/6, 7/5) and then in the final match, she achieved victory against No. 3 seed Nicole Vaidisova from the Czech Republic 6/1, 6/4. While she was already finalist at Australian Hardcourt Championships, previous Australian tournament, Peer also did a great job in doubles as she reached semi-finals with her Czech partner Jarmila Gajdosova. A girl to follow up.

Boys' Singles

All-French Boys' Final

Gaël Monfils became the fourth French to win Boys' Singles Australian Open. He defeated his friend from Insep (the place where they both train) Josselin Ouanna 6/0, 6/3 in 48 minutes. The latter was overmatched.
In the second set, 5-3, 40-15, Monfils serves for match point. He captures his first Grand Slam title with a great 128 mph serve. But 17-year-old Monfils (born on September 1, 1986) stays realistic: "I saw the names of Andy Roddick or Rod Laver on the cup – they are now pros, but I also saw names that are not in the ATP Race." It is now up to him to take the right path.

Women's Doubles

Unbreakable Pair of Ruano Pascual and Suarez

Virginia Ruano Pascual and Paola Suarez confirmed their status of world best doubles players. After beating Svetlana Kuznetsova and Elena Likhovtseva (seed No. 4) 6/4, 6/3, they captured their first doubles title in Melbourne where the Spanish-Argentine pair played their eighth consecutive Grand Slam finals together. "Our goal is to end the year as World No. 1. That's why we play all tournaments together", Ruano Pascual says.

Mixed doubles

A Nice New Pair

It was their first match together. They made a last minute partnership and that can sometimes give good results. The pair formed by the Russian Elena Bovina and the Serbian Nenad Zimonjic dominated the tournament until the end defeating defending champions Martina Navratilova and Leander Paes. "It's just great to get a trophy," Bovina said. "It doesn't matter if it's singles, doubles or mixed doubles; it's first place. It's just fantastic."

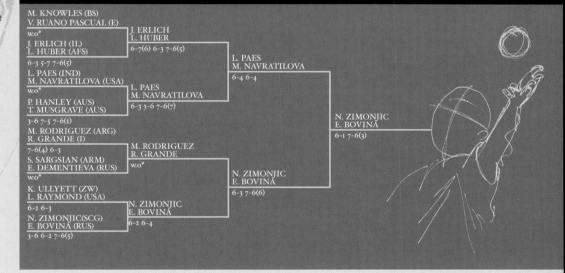

Men's doubles

Santoro-Llodra Auditioning for "The Full Monty"

A day to remember in tennis history. The French pair captures the Australian Open title for the second consecutive year. Last year, they closed the match bare-chested. So, to make it a tradition, Fabrice Santoro and Michael Llodra celebrated their second Australian victory by stripping to their underwear at Rod Laver Arena. It had been 71 years since a French team hadn't kept a Grand Slam title. The French had to fight very hard to capture this victory. In final match they defeated American world No. 1 Bryan twin brothers 7/6, 6/3. The French success is even more amazing if we take into account that Santoro was ill in bed (bronchitis – strong fever) on the morning of the fourth round.

* walkover

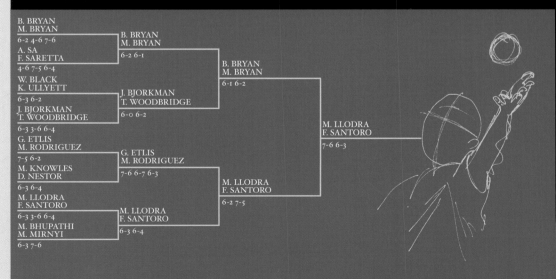

Australia Lost Its Title

Mats Wilander's team defeated the title holders in the first round. France, Netherlands, United States, Switzerland, Argentina, Spain and Belarus had been warned: they would have to count with Sweden in this competition.

France 4 - Croatia 1

Location: Metz (France)
Ground: clay court

Clement Excelled

Since he could not count on French No.1 Sebastien Grosjean, captain Guy Forget was highly criticised when he decided not to choose Fabrice Santoro, who had recently won the Australian Open in the doubles with Micheal Llodra. So, Thierry Ascione and Olivier Mutis had the opportunity to play in Metz. While Clement fulfilled his responsibilities in winning his two matches against Ancic and Ljubicic, the pair Llodra/Escude confirmed that Forget's tactical choices were right after they had won their doubles point.

The Netherlands 4 - Canada 1

Location: Maastricht (The Netherlands)
Ground: clay court

Canada Had a Hard Time

The Canadians had just joined the World Group but were to face Sjeng Schalken and Martin Verkerk, from the Netherlands. The two players respectively won their first two singles against Dancevic and Larose. The only point Canada could earn was the result of Paul Haaruis's withdrawal in the doubles. Hurt at his shoulder, he decided to put an end to his career after that match.

United States 5 - Austria 0

Location: Connecticut (United States)
Ground: hard ground

Roddick Is the Fastest Man on Earth

What could possibly be done against a team which had Andy Roddick as one of its members? Not much. Especially after the latter broke a world record with a serve reaching 150 mph! With Robby Ginepri who replaced James Blake in the singles and the Bryan brothers, one of the world best doubles team, the American team had no difficulties to qualify for the next round.

Switzerland 3 - Romania 2

Location: Bucarest (Romania)
Ground: clay court

Federer against the Romanians

Without the world No.1, who had recently won the Australian Open, the Swiss team would have had a lot of difficulties to get rid of the Romanians, led by Andrei Pavel. The three winning points were indeed won by Roger Federer, two in the singles and one in the doubles. Pavel, who was finalist in Bercy in 2003, had a break down in the last match and lost in three sets against Federer.

Argentina 5 – Marocco 0

Location: Agadir (Marocco)
Ground: GreenSet

A Clear Difference

There was nothing the Marocan team could do to avoid Younes El Aynaoui's withdrawal nor Hicham Arazi's, the national No.1, who gave up during his first match on Saturday, after having played three sets against David Nalbandian. Thanks to the point Coria captured against El Aarej and the doubles point won by the pair Arnold/Calleri against El Aarej/Tahiri, Argentina passed easily the Davis Cup first round.

Belarus 3 - Russia 2

Location: Minsk (Bielorus)
Ground: Taraflex

Voltchkov's Surprise

Vladimir Voltchkov is as cunning as a fox. He withdrew in the first match against Andreev. He seemed indeed completely unable to hit one single ball. While Max Mirnyi captured his two single matches and the Russian pair won one point, the two teams were equal on points: 2-2. On Sunday, he came back on the court to play the last match against Mikhail Youzhny. The surprise was all the more amazing since he is the one who qualified his team for the next round.

Sweden 4 – Australia 1

Location: Adelaide (Australia)
Surface: Rebound Ace

Wilander's Men Ousted the Title Holders

They had won the Davis Cup final in 2003 against Spain. The Australians did not last more than a round this year. They could not do anything against the Swedes' ardour. Philippoussis lost the first match. Hewitt equalised later. The Swedish doubles took the lead on Saturday. And Jonas Björkman, 32, eventually made his team win on Sunday, in the singles. It was a real coup de poker for the Captain Mats Wilander. Australia became the seventh title holder in the Davis Cup history to be ousted in the first round.

Spain 3 – Czech Republic 2

Location: Brno (Czech Republic)
Surface: Taraflex

Rafael Nadal is a hero

Without Carlos Moya and Juan Carlos Ferrero, the Spanish team was not too enthusiastic before playing Stepanek and Novak. While he had lost his first match on Friday against Jiri Novak, the young Rafael Nadal made amends when he brought the winning point to his country (3-2) after he defeated Radek Stepanek. Nadal highly deserved his first selection.

Opposite:
Vladimir Voltchkov

On the left:
Arnaud Clément

Davenport is Home

Lindsay Davenport has a flying season's start with a
fourth Pan Pacific Open title in Tokyo.
The 28-year-old American did not say her last words.

It feels like home to her. On Tokyo Metropolitan Gymnasium's grass, Lindsay Davenport captured the first Tier I tournament of the year for the fourth time in her career. Her first victory there was in 1998 and then the next three times she played it, in 2001, 2003, 2004 (did not attend in 2002). This year, she turned in another dominant performance to defeat unseeded Magdalena Maleeva in straight sets in the final of the Pan Pacific Open. Last time the Bulgarian was in a Tier I final was in 2002 in Moscow. She had won against... Lindsay Davenport (5/7, 6/3, 7/6).

Strengthened by her 3 Grand Slam titles (Melbourne 2000, Wimbledon 1999, Flushing Meadows 1998), the Californian girl added a 39th title to her list of awards.

She lost only 13 games during the week. Her opponents saw that as a cruel domination. After quarterfinals against Daniela Hantuchova (6/2, 6/2), the American (second-seeded) felt so good that she thought she played "my best match of the year". She played so well that she dropped only one game in semi-finals against Jelena Dokic (6/1, 6/0). As for Maleeva, she met Lisa Raymond in the first round and then another American, Laura Granville. But in quarterfinals she had to face Japanese Ai Sugiyama's audience (6/1, 6/1). Her way to the final was quite easy as she took advantage from Chanda Rubin's withdrawal (No. 5 seeded), who herself had taken advantage of Venus Williams's withdrawal.

As per Maleeva's saying, Davenport's success resulted from her serve: "Difference was made

Daniela Hantuchova

Magdalena Maleeva

in serve. Generally, she was just too good," Maleeva said. "When she is on, it's very tough to play her, because her ball is so deep in the court and she hits it so clean, and she serves well. I did pretty well, I played everything I wanted to play... every time I tried to play the point, I did not miss, I did that, so I have no regret," she said.

The American now holds a record of 12 consecutive victories in Tokyo. We can therefore believe that she feels pretty well on Japanese grass. Her fourth victory at the Toray Pan Pacific Open help Lindsay Davenport to join Conchita Martinez and Monica Seles at the first place (among players still competing in the Tour) with the highest number of Tier I tournaments victories in a career.

> " I would like to thank me for my good playing of this week. "
>
> *Magdalena Maleeva*

13

It is the number of lost games by the American Lindsay Davenport during Tokyo tournament (Tier I).

Women's Results

V. WILLIAMS (USA) 6-3 6-4			
	C. RUBIN w.o*		
C. RUBIN (USA) 7-5 6-7(3) 6-3			
		M. MALEEVA w.o*	
A. SUGIYAMA (J) 6-3 6-3			
	M. MALEEVA 6-1 6-1		
M. MALEEVA (BG) 6-1 6-3			
			L. DAVENPORT 6-4 6-1
J. DOKIC (SCG) 7-6(7) 6-7(2) 6-1			
	J. DOKIC 6-1 6-1		
T. PANOVA (RUS) 7-6(5) 6-3			
		L. DAVENPORT 6-1 6-0	
D. HANTUCHOVA (SK) 7-6(6) 6-1			
	L. DAVENPORT 6-2 6-2		
L. DAVENPORT (USA) 6-2 6-1			

* walkover

Easy for Justine

Not one set lost over this second Tier I of the season, even against Lindsay Davenport in finals. Justine Henin-Hardenne was flying on the wings of easy success that week, it was Her week.

There is no need to argue about this, Justine was dominating. Justine showed she well deserved her world No. 1 status. Not losing any set during the whole week, she won over Anastasia Myskina in the semi-finals (6/1, 6/1) and Lindsay Davenport in the final match (6/1, 6/4). Before that, Justine also got her revenge for the previous week's defeat against Svetlana Kuznetsova. The young Russian had defeated Justine in the semi-finals in Doha, Qatar. This time, the Belgian player won with a final score of 6/4, 7/5.

Anastasia Myskina

Before Californian fights started, six of the world top-ten players had withdrawn from the tournament (Mauresmo, Capriati, Williams, Dementieva, Rubin and Sugiyama). Defending champion Kim Clijsters also had to withdraw before the fourth round due to a left fist injury. Those withdrawals made the Walloon's task easier. Indeed, after her victories in Sydney, at the Australian Open and in Dubai, she won the fourth tournament of the year, the eighteenth of her career.

The best Nathalie Dechy had reached before this tournament was a third round match in a Tier I tournament. The 25-year-old French player confirmed her current top shape by reaching semi-finals and defeating players with higher rank than hers (Smashnova-Pistolesi, Zuluaga, Zvonareva).

Another player is to be congratulated, the young Gisela Dulko and her performance of the week. The 19-year-old Argentine came out of qualifications to win over two top seeds, the Spanish Maria Sanchez Lorenzo and the Russian Nadia Petrova. In the fourth round, she defeated Marissa Irvin, but eventually lost against the finalist to be, Lindsay Davenport. Nice performance for someone who is usually more specialised in doubles. Let's talk about doubles ! Let's take the same ones and start over. The doubles final in Miami was exactly the same as in the recent Australian Open. The Russian pair Kuznetsova-Likhovtseva was again defeated by the Spanish-Argentine alliance Ruano Pascual Suarez. The latter confirmed their world's leading position by crushing their opponents 6/1, 6/2.

> " I never played well here in the past. I was excited about coming back to see if things were going to be different this year. And they were. "

Justine Henin-Hardenne

O Over the whole week in Indian Wells, the Belgian tennis player Justine Henin-Hardenne did not lose one single set (as from her 1st match against Samantha Reeves until the final match against Lindsay Davenport).

Women's Results

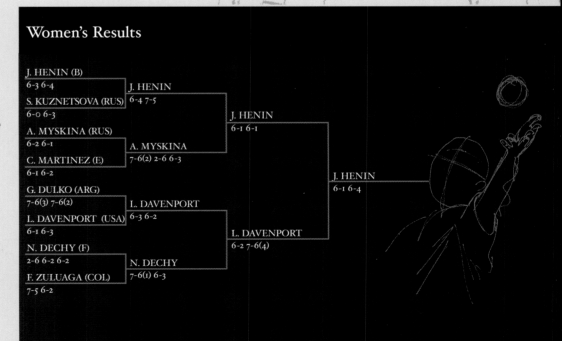

J. HENIN (B) 6-3 6-4	J. HENIN 6-4 7-5	J. HENIN 6-1 6-1		
S. KUZNETSOVA (RUS) 6-0 6-3				
A. MYSKINA (RUS) 6-2 6-1	A. MYSKINA 7-6(2) 2-6 6-3		J. HENIN 6-1 6-4	
C. MARTINEZ (E) 6-1 6-2				
G. DULKO (ARG) 7-6(3) 7-6(2)	L. DAVENPORT 6-3 6-2	L. DAVENPORT 6-2 7-6(4)		
L. DAVENPORT (USA) 6-1 6-3				
N. DECHY (F) 2-6 6-2 6-2	N. DECHY 7-6(1) 6-3			
F. ZULUAGA (COL) 7-5 6-2				

INDIAN WELLS

Tim Did Not Knock Roger Down

Federer had not won any Masters Series in 2003. This year, he captured his first ATP Master Series title of the season (second in his career) as recent world No. 1. Roger Federer confirmed his current best world rank.

But who's this longhaired guy? Roger Federer was not authorised to enter the stadium when he arrived on the site because he had no identity card with him. The security guard let him in only after having been told that he was the world No. 1, no more than that. "Roger is definitely the most popular person in Switzerland, he is their national Michael Jordan. But in the United States, it is another story!" a journalist from USA Today tried to clarify. This odd occurrence was quickly forgotten and competition could start.

It was hot there, very hot. Temperatures reached 106° Fahrenheit (41° Celsius) during the final match. On one side of

the net, we could see Roger Federer, which was not very surprising! On the other side, there was Britain's Tim Henman, who could only repeat his performance from 2002, when he was defeated by Lleyton Hewitt in the final at the same place. Henman's victories in previous matches against Larose, Corretja and Arthurs (without losing any set) were nevertheless promising, as well as the quarter-finals he won over 2003 world No. 1 Andy Roddick (6/7, 7/6, 6/3).

But Federer was not impressed by the British, one of his toughest opponents. Indeed, out of seven meetings on court between the two men, Henman has defeated him six times, including in Rotterdam last February. The only set the Swiss lost in the week was against Andre Agassi (4/6, 6/3, 6/4). Roger brushed aside Andrei Pavel, Fernando Gonzalez, Mardy Fish, Juan Ignacio Chela and Andre Agassi and claimed his first Master Series title of the season (the second of his career after Hamburg in 2002) by beating Tim Henman in 66 minutes (6/3, 6/3). "He played great," Henman said. "He certainly proved why he's the best player in the world right now". Federer also congratulated his opponent: "I think I've shown a few times that I play well against top players," Federer said. "But against Tim, it's just a different game overall just because he keeps coming to the net to hit volleys". After his victories at the Australian Open, Dubai and Indian Wells, Federer extended his ATP Race lead to 221 points over Marat Safin who holds the world second place. Tim Henman's performance allowed him to climb to ATP Race seventh seed (based on results as from January 1, 2004). Whereas no French attended the quarterfinals, Sebastien Grosjean and Arnaud Clement brilliantly captured this Master Series in doubles. Each of them had been defeated in singles: Grosjean in the fourth round and Clement in the second round, but they fought very well in doubles. They first defeated the Bryan brothers (No. 1 seed), Suk and Damm (No. 6) and the Knowles-Nestor team. Then, they won over Zimbabweans Wayne Black and Kevin Ullyet in the final match (6/3, 4/6, 7/5). The two buddies from Marseille celebrated their first doubles title together in a Masters Series.

" This was one of my goals for the season, to win an ATP Masters Series. I'm happy I won the first one because last year I couldn't win any. "

Roger Federer

Men's Results

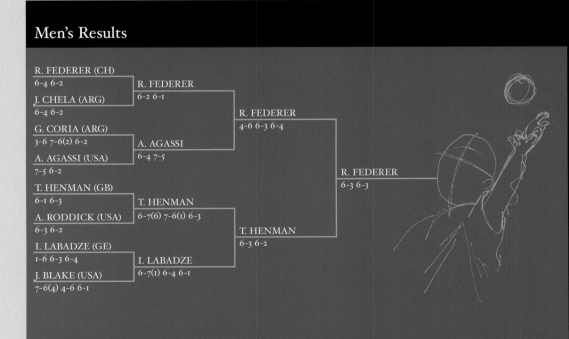

R. FEDERER (CH) 6-4 6-2	R. FEDERER 6-2 6-1		
J. CHELA (ARG) 6-4 6-2		R. FEDERER 4-6 6-3 6-4	
G. CORIA (ARG) 3-6 7-6(2) 6-2	A. AGASSI 6-4 7-5		
A. AGASSI (USA) 7-5 6-2			R. FEDERER 6-3 6-3
T. HENMAN (GB) 6-1 6-3	T. HENMAN 6-7(6) 7-6(1) 6-3		
A. RODDICK (USA) 6-3 6-2		T. HENMAN 6-3 6-2	
I. LABADZE (GE) 1-6 6-3 6-4	I. LABADZE 6-7(1) 6-4 6-1		
J. BLAKE (USA) 7-6(4) 4-6 6-1			

March 26, 2004

Serena Williams underwent a left knee surgery in August 2003, just after her victory at Wimbledon. Since then, the former world No.1 stayed away from the courts and postponed her come back several times until the D-day, Friday March 26, 2004. Since that day, things have changed, but Serena not that much.

That day, Serena Williams showed up on the tennis court and won her match. That day was Friday March 26, 2004. It was a beautiful day on the island of Key Biscayne in Florida, at the Crandon Perk Tennis Center. The fact that Serena won was nothing extraordinary in itself but it was somewhat of a performance to win so easily after such a long absence. She underwent a left knee surgery in August 2003 after which she was unable to play for some time. Her last appearance on a tennis court dated back to her victory at Wimbledon, in July

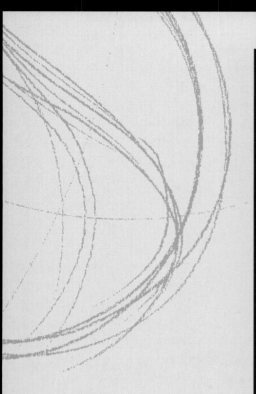

2003. This was quite a long time ago indeed. "Being my first match back, I was a little nervous going out there," admitted Serena. "But then I decided that I'm just gonna go out there, do the best I can and stay focused today." This she did in a rather brilliant way after having demolished the Spaniard Marta Marrero in forty-two minutes 6/1, 6/0. We can call it a successful comeback. And everybody was eager to see her come back. She announced it several times. First, she was to take part in the Hopman Cup (early January), then, in the Australian Open (mid-January), in the Paris Open (early February) and in Doha (late February). It finally occurred in Miami, where she had won the previous year. Serena's comeback was mainly profitable to her sponsor since she had signed a 40-million-dollar contract with Nike and could at last be seen. She showed up in Florida with a brand new white and silver silk dress, which was quite uncomfortable. "I don't have to be as comfortable as the next player!" she said. The most important is that people talk about it, this is good advertising. At Roland-Garros, a few months later, she changed and went for pink. At the US Open, even more shocking, she showed up during

warm up with a denim skirt and leather boots. Serena likes to show off.
Time had gone by very slowly with Serena being away from the court, especially for her: "Yes, I missed playing tennis a lot," she said. "During all those months, I had to be patient. I spent a lot of time with the doctors. My rehabilitation took a little longer than I expected. I wanted to come back at the Australian Open but they told me it wouldn't be proper. I listened to them and today, I know I was right," and she certainly was since she won every time she played. Serena even won the Miami title and captured another one in Beijing, late September. "To me, there's no better moment in life than a week ending with me holding a trophy a few minutes after having won a tournament. I love it because it means you're the best!" It would have been quite overenthusiastic to believe that everything would be as it was before, as when she was outplaying all players and when all of them were scared of her. During her absence, Serena lost a few ranks: she was ranked six in the world when she came back while she was at the head of the world ranking before her surgery. This is something Serena does not

"I can't wait for Kim and Justine to have recovered completely, as well as Venus and myself. It's going to be great!"

Serena Williams

> " II don't like to see a different number next to my name. "
>
> *Serena Wiliams*

accept. "The only thing I am interested in in the rankings is the first place," she said. "I do like being there and don't like to see a different number next to my name."

However, she did a lot of things while she was away from the courts. "Eight months away from the courts seemed very long even if I made the best of it and did everything I enjoy like acting and designing dresses. It was nice having time off and not having to get up at 7 to get to the courts but after a few weeks, I missed being on courts. I was watching some matches on TV telling myself that I should be on that screen." So, Serena kept herself busy. She took up acting and appeared in various soaps, among which "Law and Order". Indeed, she clearly said she would like to become a movie star. It's a little girl's dream. She is thinking about it seriously for when she retires. "Little by little, this passion grew in me and now that I am a grown up (she is now 23) and that I am thinking of my future, I just tell myself 'I am not Martina Navratilova and I won't play until 47! I will have to do something else after I retired. And since what I like most is acting, I go for it." This is probably why she decided to quit the sports agency IMG and chose William Morris, an agent from Hollywood, to manage her. Furthermore, her "boyfriend" at the time was Brett Rattner, a film producer. But Hollywood will have to wait because Serena is not quite done yet with her tennis career.

"I had to work harder to look better physically, but when you are motivated, it's not a problem and today I feel like I'm in a better shape than

last year." she said in March. But Serena is not a "machine", as Justine Henin-Hardenne would say. "The doctor said that he was shocked I was playing so many tournaments in the beginning," she said after her withdrawal at Charleston, in April. "He wondered why I decided to take part in all those tournaments one right after the other." Maybe because Serena is a fighter, she cannot help it, even though her knee is still bothering her. She is not as quick on her feet anymore, although she remains one of the most powerful players in the world. And Jelena Jankovic probably totally agrees. The Serb, whom Serena defeated in the second round in San Diego (Tier I), still remembers it: "When I first got on court I was a bit scared because she was hitting so hard. I was afraid I was going to get hit in the face. The balls were going like 300-mph. But then she wasn't hitting as hard and I knew I could play with her." As a matter fact, her serve is still very efficient. At Wimbledon, for example, she made good use of it in the fourth round against Tatiana Golovin. She served at 126 mph (her personal record). It was thanks to this excellent serve she reached the final.

So why was March 26 such an important date for the year 2004? Because Serena is not just anyone. Because she is a champion. Because she will give a lot to tennis, at least by giving it considerable media coverage. Because she makes people talk about her even out of the courts. Simply because Serena is a character, in every point of view.

Serena WILLIAMS
(Statistics dated from October 2004)

Birth date: September 6, 1981
Birthplace: Saginaw, Michigan (United States)
Height: 5'10"
Weight: 145 lb.s
Year turned pro: 1995
Best ranking: 1 (July 8 2002)
List of awards: 25 titles

2004	Miami, Beijing
2003	Australian Open, Paris (Open Gaz de France), Miami, Wimbledon
2002	Roland-Garros, Wimbledon, US Open, Miami, Scottsdale, Rome, Tokyo, Leipzig
2001	Women's Masters, Indian Wells, Canadian Open
2000	Hanover, Los Angeles, Tokyo
1999	Paris (Open Gaz de France), Indian Wells, Los Angeles, US Open, Gran Slam Cup.

Winning Return for Serena

Serena Williams had not been seen on a court since her victory at Wimbledon in 2003. The former No.1, who underwent a knee surgery in August, made her comeback in Miami to keep her title. Well done.

As if nothing had happened. As if nothing had changed. As if nine months of absence had not affected the former No.1's mind nor game. Away from the courts since July 1st due to a knee surgery scheduled for August, Serena Williams finally chose Miami to make her comeback, the comeback. She was only 6th in the world ranking but she showed up in Key Biscayne as 1st seed, with a brand new dress made of white satin and silver. She showed she could brilliantly fulfil her responsibilities in her first match against Spanish qualifier Marta Marrero. 6/1, 6/0, the whole thing was wrapped up in no more than 43 minutes and she kept such a rhythm

Opposite:
Serena Williams and Elena Dementieva

Nadia Petrova

least on the paper. She made nine double faults, which is a lot. If Serena had not "given away" her own serve in the first game and at 6/1, 5/0 when serving for the match, Elena Dementieva would have been totally humiliated. How would the audience have reacted if Serena had not been "nice" enough to give her opponent those two little games? It already booed the match several times. Serena Williams still captured 11 successive games, which is quite an achievement. The humiliation lasted for 50 minutes. The final score was harsh: 6/1, 6/1. Aged 22, Serena won the Miami tournament for the third time, a record only Steffi Graf had ever been able to accomplish (from 1994 to 1996) before.

throughout the whole tournament. She dropped only one set in the third round against Elena Likhovtseva. Serena handled, as always. So, it was hard to believe her when she said: "Two weeks ago, I was very nervous to come back here since I have not been playing for eight months." Anxiety seems to have a very good effect on her. Anastasia Myskina (seeded 3) gave up on the tournament before her first match due to a foot injury.
She was the sixth among the top 10 world players to take her name off the women's draw. Justine Henin-Hardenne and Lindsay Davenport had not even signed up for the tournament; Kim Clijsters was still recovering from a wrist injury; Jennifer Capriati, in really bad shape, did not pass the third round and Amelie Mauresmo decided not to come subsequently to her father's death.
Saturday April 3rd, 2004, Crandon Park: Serena reached the final where she played the Russian Elena Dementieva, who had managed to defeat Venus Williams in the quarterfinals. Nothing too hard for the American tennis player. Dementieva did not win one single serving game during this one-way final. This is quite worrisome at such a high level, especially knowing she is the eighth "best player in the world", at

265

Serena Williams only showed up on a court 265 days after her victory at Wimbledon. This was in Key Biscayne, Florida. The knee surgery she underwent in August had forced her to rest.

" I had to work harder than ever to be in good shape, but when you are motivated, it is not a problem. I think that I am in better shape than last year. "

Serena Williams

Women's Results

S. WILLIAMS (USA) 6-4 6-3				
	S. WILLIAMS 6-0 6-1			
J. CRAYBAS (USA) 4-6 6-4 7-6(2)				
		S. WILLIAMS 6-4 6-4		
E. DANIILIDOU (GR) 7-6(8) 6-1				
	E. DANIILIDOU 6-1 6-3			
K. SPREM (HR) 3-6 7-5 6-4				
			S. WILLIAMS 6-1 6-1	
N. PETROVA (RUS) 6-2 6-1				
	N. PETROVA 6-2 6-2			
N. DECHY (F) 6-3 6-2				
		E. DEMENTIEVA 6-4 6-2		
E. DEMENTIEVA (RUS) 5-7 6-1 6-3				
	E. DEMENTIEVA 6-3 5-7 7-6(3)			
V. WILLIAMS (USA) 6-1 6-3				

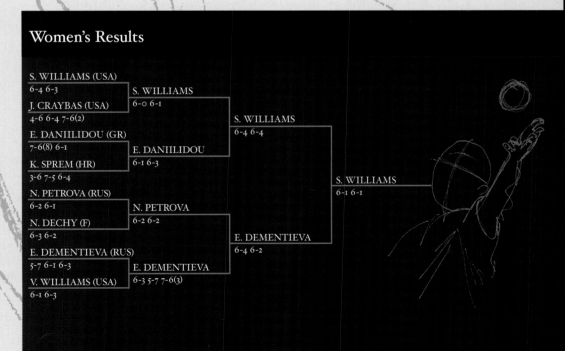

Coria Let Roddick Win

The Argentine Guillermo Coria was forced to retire due to back spasms and therefore, conceded victory to Andy Roddick. The American captured the thirteenth title of his career in Miami.

"At the beginning, it was just the serve. Then as I progressed, it started hurting on every side, sitting down, standing up. I knew it was very difficult to play Roddick feeling this way", Coria explained. He could have stopped after the first set he won (7/6). "But nobody wants to give up at that time, in such a tournament's final match, with so many people who paid to come and watch me!" he commented. That's why Coria, who was playing his second final on a hard court, went on playing and put on a show for the audience, i.e. 13,118 spectators, mostly Americans and Spaniards, who make Florida's population. But Coria's back pain was excruciating.

He was forced to give up for good after 2.01 hours of match (6/7, 6/3, 6/1). Andy Roddick captured the Miami Masters Series. It's the third Masters Series he wins in his career (after Montreal and Cincinnati in 2003), his second title in 2004 and his two-hundredth match in the ATP Tour. Aged 21, Andy Roddick became the youngest winner of a tournament since Michael Chang in 1992.

It is the third time in 20 years that this tournament's final match ends with one of the opponents' withdrawal. In 1989, Thomas Muster was unable to play due to a car accident that occurred a few hours after he won his semi-final match. In 1996, Goran Ivanisevic woke up with a stiff neck the morning of the final and had to give up in the first set against Andre Agassi.

Other players were unlucky for the second Masters Series of the season. First of all, Roger Federer, the recent Indian Wells winner, who was upset by the young fiery Rafael Nadal (17 years old). It was the first time since August 2003 and the Cincinnati Masters Series that the world No. 1 lost without making it to the last sixteen.

Another shocking news was the defeat in the fourth round of the American player, Andre Agassi, against the Argentine Agustin Calleri. A few days before his 34th birthday, the six-times Miami champ would have liked to capture this title for the fourth time consecutively.

Andy Roddick

> " Guillermo slowed by an injury is still faster than about 90 percent of the guys on the Tour "
>
> *Andy Roddick*

9

After hitting a forehand into the net in the 9th game of the final against Andy Roddick, the Argentine Guillermo Coria felt a sharp pain in the back, which forced him to retire from the match.

Men's Results

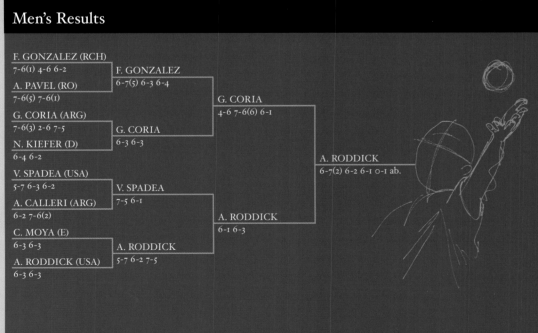

F. GONZALEZ (RCH) 7-6(1) 4-6 6-2	F. GONZALEZ 6-7(5) 6-3 6-4		
A. PAVEL (RO) 7-6(5) 7-6(1)		G. CORIA 4-6 7-6(6) 6-1	
G. CORIA (ARG) 7-6(3) 2-6 7-5	G. CORIA 6-3 6-3		
N. KIEFER (D) 6-4 6-2			A. RODDICK 6-7(2) 6-2 6-1 0-1 ab.
V. SPADEA (USA) 5-7 6-3 6-2	V. SPADEA 7-5 6-1		
A. CALLERI (ARG) 6-2 7-6(2)		A. RODDICK 6-1 6-3	
C. MOYA (E) 6-3 6-3	A. RODDICK 5-7 6-2 7-5		
A. RODDICK (USA) 6-3 6-3			

DAVIS CUP

The Frenchmen Defeated the Giant Federer

The French team defeated Switzerland and world No.1 Roger Federer, not without any trouble. France's next opponent will be Spain, who were playing the United States in the other quarterfinal.

France 3 – Switzerland 2

Location: Prilly (Switzreland)
Surface: Opticourt

The French Revenge

Guy Forget's team still remembered its humiliation last year, at the same stage of the competition, in front of the same Swiss. There were some differences though: French No.1 Sebastien Grosjean did not join the team this year and the other big difference with 2003 was Roger Federer. Being world No.1, he logically won his two singles matches.

While Arnaud Clement evened on the first day (1-1) defeating Ivo Heuberger, the doubles match eventually made the difference. The pair Escude/Llodra played particularly well against Allegro and Federer. Nicolas Escude had then the responsibility of capturing the winning point in the fifth and last match, which he did against Michel Kratochvil. So it reminds anybody that one single man cannot make a whole team win, even if this man is called Roger Federer.

Spain 4 – The Netherlands 1

Location: Palma de Mallorca (Spain)
Surface: red clay
The Champions Made Their Comeback
This time, Carlos Moya and Juan Carlos Ferrero did join the team, unlike in the first round, which was a very good thing for Spain since they brought the first two points to their country. On Friday, they indeed defeated Martin Verkerk and Raemon Sluiter without losing a set. One single point was then enough to qualify. The pair Rafael Nadal/Tommy Robredo was in charge of bringing that winning point to their country. After they had won the first two sets, the rain interrupted the match, which was postponed on the next day. The pair Van Lottum/Verkerk took advantage of this mishap and came back to eventually win in five sets. Ferrero also needed five sets against Verkerk to capture the winning point.

Martin Verkerk and
John Van Lottum

United States 4 – Sweden 1

Location: Delray Beach (United States)
Surface: Plexiplave
The Davis Cup Is Synonym of Record for Roddick
The Swedes could not repeat their first round performance in which they defeated title holder Australia. This time, they were facing a rather strong American team, which was as powerful as the serve of its leader, Andy Roddick. After having broken the world fastest serve record in the first round against Austria, he broke his own record. It is now possible to serve at 152 mph! Unless he is the only one who can do it… With a much weaker serve, Mardy and the Bryan brothers also contributed towards the US easy victory.

Belarus 5 – Argentina 0

Location: Minsk (Belarus)
Surface: Taraflex
The Belarusians Were Surprising
They only dropped one set in five matches (in the last singles match which could not change anything). Belarus was clearly superior to a weakened Argentina. Guillermo Coria and David Nalbandian's absences did have big consequences. This performance is to be attributed to two men: Vladimir Voltchkov and Max Mirnyi, who played two singles each and who even paired up to play the doubles. It was the first time in the Davis Cup history that Belarus reached the semi-finals. The next stage was to be Charleston, in the United States, in Andy Roddick's kingdom. Things were getting harder and harder for them but anyway, the Belarusians were not expected so far in the competition. So why not a third performance in a row? Let's wait for the semi-finals in September.

It Was so Long Ago...

It had been a long time since Venus Williams had not captured a title. She reactivated her list of awards on clay court in Charleston, South Carolina.

South Carolina was the witness of many last-minute withdrawals, including seed No. 1 Justine Henin-Hardenne and seed No. 3 Amelie Mauresmo. Justine felt physically too weak. The constant weariness she had felt for two weeks was diagnosed as low blood sugar (hypoglycaemia) resulting in dizziness. "I have felt bad for two weeks now and that's enough. I will now go back home and do everything I have in order to get better."

Venus Williams

Mauresmo preferred not to take the risk of getting injured because of the fatigue she accumulated in Amelia Island, where she was defeated in final against Davenport. The French could still feel some discomfort in her back. Suffering from both knees, Serena Williams (top seed No.2) also decided to withdraw in the fourth round before meeting Conchita Martinez. All those withdrawals served well Venus Williams and Conchita Martinez in their way up to the final. Venus had not reached a final since 2003 in Wimbledon, where she was defeated by her sister. Their last match together dated from the quarterfinals in San Diego in 2000. (Venus won 6/3, 6/0.) This time, the match was tight. Venus appeared to be the first in trouble and lost the first set. It is only at the beginning of the second set that the American woke up. She actually woke up in time and ended up winning 2/6, 6/2, 6/1. "I did not find my top game

> " In my whole career, I've never received this much support anywhere. It took me a while to get used to it! "
>
> *Venus Wiliams*

14

14 months ago, Venus won her last tournament. The former No. 1 put an end to this lack of victories by winning the thirtieth title of her career, in Charleston.

back, but it is work in progress", she admitted later. With thirty titles, Venus became the 13th player having won the highest number of tournaments (since Open era's beginning). The other finalist, Conchita Martinez is the 11th on this list with thirty-two titles. The Spanish girl also became the seventh player in the ranking by number of total victories with a total of 700 wins. Those are pretty nice statistics but they remain 'weak' if we compare them with Martina Navratilova's 1440 victories. By the way, let's say a few words about Martina Navratilova! After her doubles final match defeat with Lisa Raymond against the Ruano Pascual – Suarez team (6/4, 6/1), she announced that she would retire at the end of the year. The American also took part in the Charleston singles for the thirteenth time in her career. The one who has won this event four times was eliminated on the first round by Amy Frazier 6/4, 6/4. Would the 47-year-old woman (finally) be getting tired?

Conchita Martinez

Jelena Kostanic

* walkover

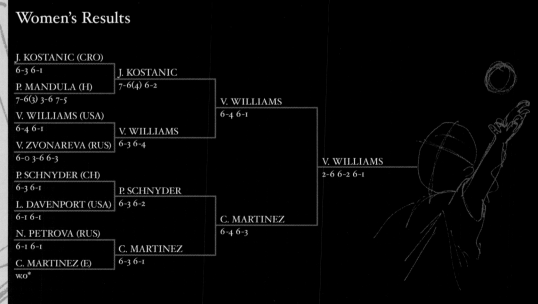

Women's Results

J. KOSTANIC (CRO) 6-3 6-1				
	J. KOSTANIC 7-6(4) 6-2			
P. MANDULA (H) 7-6(3) 3-6 7-5				
		V. WILLIAMS 6-4 6-1		
V. WILLIAMS (USA) 6-4 6-1				
	V. WILLIAMS 6-3 6-4			
V. ZVONAREVA (RUS) 6-0 3-6 6-3				
			V. WILLIAMS 2-6 6-2 6-1	
P. SCHNYDER (CH) 6-3 6-1				
	P. SCHNYDER 6-3 6-2			
L. DAVENPORT (USA) 6-1 6-1				
		C. MARTINEZ 6-4 6-3		
N. PETROVA (RUS) 6-1 6-1				
	C. MARTINEZ 6-3 6-1			
C. MARTINEZ (E) w.o*				

MONTE-CARLO

Coria All Red

The Argentine Guillermo Coria, who is a specialist on clay, honoured the first great European event on this surface with his presence. He beat an amazing Rainer Schuettler in the final, achieving his 26th consecutive victory on red clay.

His name is Guillermo Coria, he is 22 years old, he is a tennis player and he loves red clay. This is the short story that describes the new Monte-Carlo Open winner (in the absence of Roger Federer and Andy Roddick, world Nos. 1 and 2). The Argentine's endurance pushed out of competition players such as Thomas Enqvist, Nicolas Kiefer, Andrei Pavel, David Nalbandian and Marat Safin, one after the other. Even the German's strength of Rainer Schuettler could not resist Coria's persistence in the final match. Although the German was

26 Thanks to his final match against Rainer Schuettler in Monte-Carlo, the Argentine Guillermo now holds a total of 26 consecutive victories on red clay since 2003 Roland-Garros (defeated in semi-finals by Verkerk).

Marat Safin

celebrating his 28th birthday, Guillermo Coria, already finalist last year, did not intend to give him any kind of present as the final result confirms: 6/2, 6/1, 6/3. But the result of this match did not reflect that week's reality. "I was prepared to play a very long match and very long points, but, in fact, the result doesn't really reflect what it was on the court because every game was very tight", Coria said. Despite a slight injury, Schuettler eliminated Gustavo Kuerten, Jean-René Lisnard, Lleyton Hewitt, Tim Henman and Carlos Moya (three former world No. 1!). The German reached a final match in Masters Series for the first time in his career. Coria, who was unlucky in last year's finals against Juan Carlos Ferrero, won his second Masters Series (after Hamburg in

2003), the eighth tournament of his career. Therefore, he advanced to the third rank in the Race.

Ferrero was expected to do better than he did, at least in the last four. Winner in 2002 and 2003, Juan Carlos Ferrero was defeated 6/2, 6/3 in the first round by his fellow Alex Corretja. In a victory scenario, he would have entered the tournament's history, joining the private society of three times winners Björn Borg, Thomas Muster, Ilie Nastase and Guillermo Vilas.

Gustavo Kuerten was also expected to still be in competition at the end of the week. But the double winner of this event remained stuck in the first round defeated by Schuettler (7/6, 6/3), like Ferrero.

" I hope to follow in the footsteps of Juan Carlos Ferrero and Guga, who won first Monte-Carlo and then Roland-Garros. But what I will do is to think about one match at a time. And if I fail, I won't be too hard on myself. "

Guillermo Coria

Men's Results

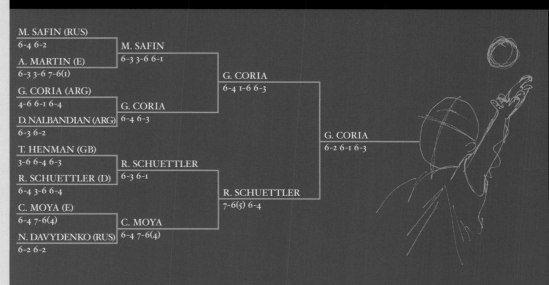

M. SAFIN (RUS) 6-4 6-2	M. SAFIN 6-3 3-6 6-1			
A. MARTIN (E) 6-3 3-6 7-6(1)		G. CORIA 6-4 1-6 6-3		
G. CORIA (ARG) 4-6 6-1 6-4	G. CORIA 6-4 6-3			
D. NALBANDIAN (ARG) 6-3 6-2			G. CORIA 6-2 6-1 6-3	
T. HENMAN (GB) 3-6 6-4 6-3	R. SCHUETTLER 6-3 6-1			
R. SCHUETTLER (D) 6-4 3-6 6-4		R. SCHUETTLER 7-6(5) 6-4		
C. MOYA (E) 6-4 7-6(4)	C. MOYA 6-4 7-6(4)			
N. DAVYDENKO (RUS) 6-2 6-2				

Who Does the Cup Go To?

2004 Fed Cup has started. At home, on the clay courts of the " Coliseum d'Amiens ", reigning Fed Cup champions France easily dominated the young German team. Only the United States went home with a victory. Austria, Russia, Belgium, Spain, Italy and Argentine also made it to the next round.

France 5 – Germany 0

Place: Amiens (France)
Surface: clay court
Stormy Mauresmo
Even if world No. 100 Nathalie Dechy was on a rocky road throughout the match against Anna-Lena Groenefeld, she turned the match upside down (6/7, 6/1, 6/4) so France could defeat a young German team. Amelie Mauresmo, who stormed through the second rubber, brought the next 2 necessary points for victory. Emilie Loit (victory against Schruff 6/2, 6/2) and the pair Dechy-Mauresmo did utmost to close the week-end the best way (5 - 0).

USA 4 – Slovenia 1

Place: Portoroz (Slovenia)
Surface: clay court
No Serena, No Lindsay, No Jennifer
Despite the absence of Serena Williams, Lindsay Davenport and Jennifer Capriati, the United States assured their qualification, beating Slovenia. Only Lisa Raymond was not top fit. She lost the first singles match against Tina Pisnik 7/5, 7/5. But Venus Williams threw a wrench into Slovenia's hopes. The pair Navratilova/Raymond could then bring the last point without feeling any pressure.

Austria 3 – Slovakian Republic 2

Place: St.-Pölten (Austria)
Surface: clay court
Barbara Schett Did Not Give Up
It was not so easy for Barbara Schett (Austria's leader) but easy enough anyway to defeat Janette Husarova (4/6, 6/1, 6/4). The next two matches were also taken by Austria, including another Schett's three-set victory against world No. 54 Martina Sucha. The last two meetings were not to be taken into account for qualification (2 victories for Slovenia).

Russia 4 – Austria 1

Place: Moscow (Russia)
Surface: Taraflex
Wealthy Russia
Victories of both Svetlana Kuznetsova and Anastasia Myskina over Alicia Molik and Samantha Stosur put Russia in a very comfortable position as from Saturday. Beating Myskina (6/3, 6/3) the day after, Alicia Molik only postponed the final Russian victory thanks to Vera Zvonareva, who sealed a victory that qualified her.

Argentine 4 – Japan 1

Place: Buenos Aires (Argentine)
Surface: clay court
Powerless Sugiyama
The Japanese women did not pose a threat on Argentine's Gisela Dulko and Paola Suarez's victory. The world No. 10 Ai Sugiyama (playing Suarez) had to give up in the decisive set due to cramps. That set turned out to be the tightest of the week-end. Morigami's victory over Dulko could not influence the qualification.

Spain 3 – Switzerland 2

Place: Los Belones (Spain)
Surface: clay court
In-Form Martinez Makes the Difference
All square on Saturday as both Conchita Martinez and Patty Schnyder won their duels. The two singles of the next day resulted in a tie. The victory point was therefore caught by the Spanish pair formed by the specialist Virginia Ruano Pascual and Conchita Martinez.

Opposite: Kim Clijsters

Belgium 3 – Croatia 2

Place: Bree (Belgium)
Surface: clay court
No Henin But a Decisive Callens
Justine Henin-Hardenne was not there. Therefore, Kim Clijsters had the role of key player for Belgium. And she performed very well. Indeed, the Flemish girl won her two singles matches against Jelena Kostanic and then Karolina Sprem. But the decisive point was brought by Els Callens. At the age of 33, she was preferred to Kirsten Flipkens to play the last singles match in three sets against Kostanic.

Italia 3 – Czech Republic 1

Place: Lecce (Italy)
Surface: clay court
It Was Hard but Italy is Through To Quarterfinals!
Francesca Schiavione lost each first set of each match to further win over all her opponents. She won her two singles matches. Strycova brings the single Czech point. The match Schiavone-Koukalova was postponed to Monday due to rain. As Italy was certain of being through to the World Group Quarterfinals, both coaches agreed not to come the day after.

Amélie Mauresmo and Guy Forget

One Set from Perfection

The Spaniard Carlos Moya lost only one set in the fourth tour of the tournament. Defeating the Argentine David Nalbandian, he won a third Master Series in his career, a second one on clay ground.

On Italian clay, Carlos Moya rolled up his sleeves far above the elbow to finish off (quite easily) Alberto Martin, Ivan Ljubicic, Andrei Pavel and the Croatian Ivo Karlovic. Only the latter managed to tickle him, in the fourth round, being the only one to take one set from him. Moya stated "The only match I had trouble in was against Karlovic because he doesn't give a rhythm to the ball. I have been very close to losing. But after I won the match, I realised I was playing well."

He then never stopped playing well until the final (his fifth in five months) during which he won 60% of the points on Nalbadian's first serve. It's therefore logical that Nalbadian was defeated in three sets 6/3, 6/3, 6/1.

On the left:
Carlos Moya

David Nalbandian

Though he had never reached the quarterfinals in Rome, Moya succeeded to another Spaniard, Felix Mantilla. The Argentine happened to be the only seed (nr 5) to meet Moya. Indeed, two of the largest favourites fell prematurely: Roger Federer (ranked 1st) who got stuck in the second tour against Albert Costa (3/6, 6/3, 6/2) and Andy Roddick (ranked 2nd) who did not even pass the first tour after a harsh defeat against Guillermo Canas (7/6, 6/1).

Thanks to his recent good results – one title in Chennai, Acapulco, and two finals in Sydney and Buenos Aires, Moya surges from the fifth to the second rank in the Race. David Nalbandian, for his part, makes a nice move in the ranking, rocketing from the 22nd rank to the 8th. Moya latest victory has for a result that the first four ranked in the Race are the winners of the first four Masters Series of the year: Roger Federer (Indian Wells), Andy Roddick (Miami), Guillermo Coria (Monte Carlo) and Moya (Rome). Carlos Moya, 27 years old, won the seventeenth title in his career and his third Masters Series after Monte Carlo in 1998 and Cincinnati in 2002.

The story

It's Been Getting Hot in Rome

Saturday, May 3, 5.15 am. Two American tourists dump a cigarette butt in the bin of room 305 in Rome's 5-starred hotel Parco dei Principi. The same hotel that also hosts players such as Andy Roddick, Sjeng Schalken, Mariano Zabaleta, Max Mirnyi or Marat Safin. The bin starts burning and the flames spread over the whole building. The 350 customers are subsequently evacuated from the hotel, including the players who have to leave bags and rackets behind.

Filipo Volandri (ranked 53) told journalists "I have been roughly awoke by the smoke and not by the security alarm which did not work. The whole room turned black filled with smoke. I opened the door and realised it was impossible to get out in the hallway. I then locked myself out of the room on the balcony. The firemen eventually got me out through a nacelle." Andy Roddick also had quite an adventure: "When I woke up to go to the loo, it smelled like burnt. When I opened the door, a cloud of black smoke spread into the room. I went on the balcony and saw Sjeng Schalken and his wife on the seventh floor. There were four tourists and one Italian with them. They jumped on my balcony and we all waited there. It was very strange, especially when knowing that some people on our floor have been asphyxiated to death…"

" The conditions were not easy for me. It rained a lot, several days, I came here at 9 am, and left at 11 pm. "

Carlos Moya

5

Moya, who has appeared in five final matches on five continents in the first five months of the season, surges from fifth to second in the INDESIT ATP 2004 Race.

Men's Results

A. COSTA (E) 6-2 6-3	A. COSTA 6-4 6-2		
J. NOVAK (CZ) 6-3 7-5		D. NALBANDIAN 6-7(4) 6-1 6-4	
V. SPADEA (USA) 4-6 6-3 6-4	D. NALBANDIAN 6-4 6-3		
D. NALBANDIAN (ARG) 7-6(4) 3-6 6-4			C. MOYA 6-3 6-3 6-1
N. MASSU (RCH) 7-5 6-4	M. ZABALETA 6-1 7-5		
M. ZABALETA (ARG) 3-6 6-3 6-2		C. MOYA 6-3 6-4	
C. MOYA (E) 6-4 3-6 6-4	C. MOYA 6-1 6-2		
A. PAVEL (RO) 7-6(3) 7-6(5)			

A No Pain Victory

After Venus Williams's withdrawal from the final, Amelie Mauresmo captures her first title of the Tour, laying down on her sofa in a hotel. Mind as well, it still is a victory.

"There is a huge difference in winning a final title on the court or winning it from a sofa in a hotel." Anyway, Amelie Mauresmo got it and there is no more to it. Even if she won it thanks to Venus Williams' withdrawal, this is also part of sport. And her week remains really great, especially after her semi-final match against previous No. 1 Jennifer Capriati, who was severely defeated in 53 minutes 6-2, 6-0. She lost only one set in one week, against Svetlana Kuznetsova (top tenth-seed) in quarter-finals (6-7, 6-3, 6-1).
When she tells journalists after the match that she feels top fit and has new sensations, everyone believes her.

On the final's morning, Venus Williams makes her withdrawal from the Tour official. The day before, she had sprained her foot when passing shot at the 4th point of the last game of semi-final against the Croatian Karolina Sprem (2-6, 6-3, 6-4). Diagnosis : pulled ligament in her left ankle. She left Berlin for the United States on crutches. Too bad for her. Too bad for Amelie. Too bad for the tournament, which was celebrating its 108th anniversary.

But Venus's withdrawal is not the only one of the week. An upper arm problem saw Patty Schnyder's withdraw, and the Belgian Kim

On the left: Capriati and Mauresmo

Amélie Mauresmo   Venus Wiliams

Clijsters as well. She gave up after her victory in the first round against Maria Marrero due to a painful left fist. This injury even made her give up on Roland-Garros, Wimbledon and the US Open. "Professional tennis becomes harder and harder", French No. 1 explains. "Level is higher and higher every year. We have to work harshly to follow up. But sometimes the body gives up. "

Amelie Mauresmo also hesitated to withdraw from tournament due to chronic back pain. "On Sunday, during training, my back was painful, she explains. I was not sure to play till the morning of my first match (on Wednesday against Dulko). And one week later, here I am, with an award in hands…Funny, isn't it?"

Her mantle piece is also very happy about it. Amelie may now display another 'Silver Bear' on it. She had already won this title in Berlin in 2001. It is the 11th title she wins in her career, the first of the year.

An exhibition match has been arranged for German fans between the 'already champion' and No. 5 seed Anastasia Myskina, who had reached quarterfinals in single draw and semi-finals in double. Since no real final was to be fought, this was much better than nothing.

> " It is quite strange to win a title without playing. I am a bit disappointed as I wanted to play one more match. "
>
> *Amélie Mauresmo*

2 It is the Amelie Mauresmo's 2nd victory at Ladies German Open. She had captured this title in 2001 against Capriati and reached final in 1998 (defeated by Conchita Martinez).

*walkover

Women's Results

K. SPREM (CRO) w.o*				
	K. SPREM 6-3 6-3			
F. ZULUAGA (COL) 7-6(3) 3-6 6-4				
		V. WILLIAMS 2-6 6-3 6-4		
V. WILLIAMS (USA) 6-3 6-1				
	V. WILLIAMS 7-6(5) 5-7 6-2			
P. SUAREZ (ARG) 6-1 7-6(6)				
			A. MAURESMO w.o*	
J. CAPRIATI (USA) 5-7 6-4 6-1				
	J. CAPRIATI 6-3 6-2			
A. MYSKINA (RUS) w.o**				
		A. MAURESMO 6-2 6-0		
S. KUZNETSOVA (RUS) 6-2 6-7(5) 6-4				
	A. MAURESMO 6-7(7) 6-3 6-1			
A. MAURESMO (F) 6-2 6-7(5) 6-4				

Federer Hits Back

No. 1 World player Roger Federer proved once again he could be dangerous on all grounds as his second victory on Hamburg's clay ground confirms it.

He can still remember it. It was in 2002, on the same clay ground in Hamburg, that Roger Federer won his first Masters Series in his career by defeating Marat Safin. He was then only 20 years old. This time, the Swiss had to play a clay expert in this most expected final opposing the World-ranked No. 1 and the titleholder Guillermo Coria (seeded no. 2). Though the Swiss was not one of the large favourites on clay tournaments, this week, he brilliantly managed to win over Gaston Gaudio (who later won Roland-Garros), Nicolas Lapentti, Fernando Gonzalez, Carlos Moya, Lleyton Hewitt and last but not least, Guillermo Coria, all great clay ground players.

boasting his first performance: "I had already played very well that week in Hamburg, defeating top players like Kuerten or Safin." With several victories at the Australian Open, in Dubai and in two Masters Series: Indian Wells and Hamburg, Federer has taken a comfortable lead in the Race, in front of Carlos Moya. It was Coria's first defeat on clay since Roland Garros semi-final match against Martin Verkerk in 2003. "Of course I am disappointed because the finals are for sure the matches we hate most to lose when playing at this level." He could cheer up once he reached the 3rd ranking in the Race, thanks to two Masters Series finals (Miami and Hamburg) and a victory in the TMS Monte Carlo. "There is nothing to be ashamed of. I have just lost against the No.1. There is a reason why he is currently the best player in the world!"

" Sometimes it is more difficult to win a second time. For me it's an unbelievable surprise that I can win this tournament twice in such a young career. "

Roger Federer

31

Guillermo Coria

Roger Federer put an end to Guillermo Coria's impressive series of 31 victories in a row on clay ground. The Argentine's last defeat on this ground dates back to June 2003 (semi-finals in Roland-Garros against Verkerk).

A little reminder: Coria and Federer already played the Orange Bowl's final in 1998. Federer won, which was an extra motivation for the Argentine to win the match and keep his title. He was confident from the start as he broke as soon as the first game had been played. Hope grew stronger after winning the first set in about thirty minutes. Before that, Federer had given us much to worry about with a first serve rate of 36%. Did it have anything to do with the fact that he stayed up late the night before? – He went to the Britney Spears' show to please his girlfriend. This obviously made him tired enough to lose the first set. Hurt in his pride, the Swiss finally woke up and ended the match in 2.20 hours and four sets (4/6, 6/4, 6/2, 6/3).

Roger jokes about the tennis he's been playing since his first victory in Hamburg: "Listen, it is quite simple, I do almost everything a little bit better than two years ago." Nonetheless

Men's Results

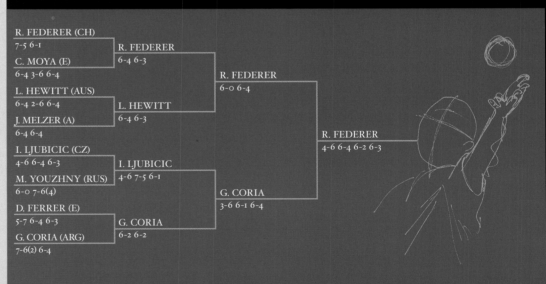

R. FEDERER (CH) 7-5 6-1			
	R. FEDERER 6-4 6-3		
C. MOYA (E) 6-4 3-6 6-4		R. FEDERER 6-0 6-4	
L. HEWITT (AUS) 6-4 2-6 6-4			
	L. HEWITT 6-4 6-3		R. FEDERER 4-6 6-4 6-2 6-3
J. MELZER (A) 6-4 6-4			
I. LJUBICIC (CZ) 4-6 6-4 6-3			
	I. LJUBICIC 4-6 7-5 6-1		
M. YOUZHNY (RUS) 6-0 7-6(4)		G. CORIA 3-6 6-1 6-4	
D. FERRER (E) 5-7 6-4 6-3			
	G. CORIA 6-2 6-2		
G. CORIA (ARG) 7-6(2) 6-4			

Two in a Row

The French tennis player Amelie Mauresmo stamped her authority on the clay court circuit, winning in Berlin her second title in 2004, the twelfth in her career. With two titles in two weeks, she warms up nicely ahead of Roland-Garros in France.

Amelie falls to her knees. She just won the Women's clay court Italian Open, beating the American Jennifer Capriati in a two-and-a-half hour match. The American was fighting much harder than at the semi-finals the week before in Berlin (6-2, 6-0). World No. 3 even had to play her way out of match point before winning 3/6, 6/3, 7/6. This is her fourth final appearance in Rome (after 2000, 2001, 2003) and her first victory.

At the age of 24, Mauresmo equals Steffi Graf and Monica Seles's records, who were the only ones to have performed

Amélie Mauresmo

such a record (Graf in 1987 and Seles in 1990), taking the successive titles in Berlin and Rome (2 Tier I). To have the comparison right, Amelie now has to imitate their Grand Slam victories. Please note that Graf and Seles had also won Roland-Garros just after. Unfortunately it won't be the case for the French, not yet.

Despite her No. 3 ranking (behind Justine Henin-Hardenne and Kim Clijsters), ranking No. 1 had been given to Serena Williams, who was 4 ranks behind her. The American still slightly suffers from her left knee. She will be bothered by

this pain the whole week and won't be able to play her best tennis. "It was a struggle today. I hit a lot of fly balls. I couldn't hit the ball in . I am still wondering why ! I probably made 1000 direct faults", she admits after her second round struggling match against Maria Sanchez Lorenzo.

But in the semi-finals Top No. 1 was severely defeated by Jennifer Capriati. The latter was appearing for the 1st time in final in Rome, after 14 years of career. Better late than never.

Vera Zvonareva

" My victories helped me a lot and were good for my self-confidence. I thought: all the attention will be drawn on me at Roland-Garros, so it is better to win before that! "

Amélie Mauresmo

4

Defeated in the semi-final match in the Rome tournament, Serena Williams could enjoy doing some shopping. She bought 4 handbags, whereas she had already 20 of them in her luggage when she arrived in Italy.

Women's Results

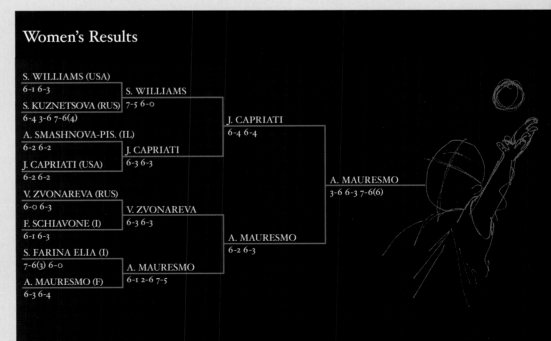

Round 1	Round 2	Quarterfinal	Semifinal	Final
S. WILLIAMS (USA) 6-1 6-3	S. WILLIAMS 7-5 6-0			
S. KUZNETSOVA (RUS) 6-4 3-6 7-6(4)		J. CAPRIATI 6-4 6-4		
A. SMASHNOVA-PIS. (IL) 6-2 6-2	J. CAPRIATI 6-3 6-3			
J. CAPRIATI (USA) 6-2 6-2			A. MAURESMO 3-6 6-3 7-6(6)	
V. ZVONAREVA (RUS) 6-0 6-3	V. ZVONAREVA 6-3 6-3			
F. SCHIAVONE (I) 6-1 6-3		A. MAURESMO 6-2 6-3		
S. FARINA ELIA (I) 7-6(3) 6-0	A. MAURESMO 6-1 2-6 7-5			
A. MAURESMO (F) 6-3 6-4				

Russia's Sovereignty

The two "Tsarinas" of the French Open were quite unexpected. Anastasia Myskina and Elena Dementieva indeed created a surprising effect. Myskina is the first Russian woman to win a Grand Slam. She is certainly not the last one.

"No two years are ever the same." Well, almost! For the first time since tennis exists, a Russian woman captured a Grand Slam title. This Russian is called Anastasia Myskina. But the winner could also have been called Elena Dementieva. These two 22-year-old players actually faced each other in the Roland-Garros final match. This was a first time in history, even if we had seen two women from the same country fighting for the same title before. In 2003, Justine Henin-Hardenne was meeting Kim Clijsters for the first all-Belgian final. Russia and Belgium are not the only countries that experienced it: the USA did twelve times, Australia three times and France once. But this time, this all-Russian final should be history quite quickly because it was of no interest at all. Thirty-three unforced errors committed by Dementieva. Even the match point was not a nice one. "I didn't really remember. I mean, it was out, but then everybody was quiet, and I was quiet. I was like, I don't know, maybe that was double-fault or something, Myskina admitted later. Then I realised that I had just captured a Grand Slam title. An extraordinary dream came true." As for

"
This final match was so important for both of us that I did not want to increase her disappointment by screaming my happiness. "

Anastasia Myskina

"
I was so nervous, so sad. I could not see the ball clearly. I could not calm down out here. No it was not me on the court today. "

Elena Dementieva

Anastasia Myskina

Dementieva, it was a nightmare: "I was so nervous, so sad. I could not see the ball clearly. I could not calm down out there. No, it was not me on the court today, I could not play my game." Fortunately for her, this nightmare ended after only 58 minutes.

Myskina won. She managed better in this battle of nerves. If this final remains historic, it is only thanks to the fact that it was an all-Russian event. On the court, neither of the two girls played their best tennis. The long-term friends have known each other since they were 7. They used to train together at the Spartak in Moscow. When they were kids, they used to play for pizza and now, a few years later, as the new champion put it, she has won the "biggest" pizza of all (indeed the prize amounts to 838,500 euros). With this title, Myskina, who had won only one match in Roland-Garros so far, climbed directly from the fifth world rank to the third, her best ranking so far. Despite this poor last match, Myskina may be proud of having defeated Venus Williams and Jennifer Capriati before the final. "I think the key was Molik match for me because I lost Alicia just a couple months ago, something, the Fed Cup in Moscow. And when I came here, I was just like thinking to go and play against Alicia. And then, of course, after this match I get a lot of confidence in myself.

Anastasia Myskina and
Elena Dementieva

Early Exit for Martina

Values are not what they were anymore. The "old" ones are not respected anymore. After Andre Agassi's first round exit at the hands of France's 271-ranked Jerome Haenel, Martina Navratilova was ousted in the same round by Gisela Dulko 6/1, 6/3. It is one of the worse results for the American in a Grand Slam. She has captured a total of 167 titles in singles (including 18 Grand Slam's ones) and 173 in doubles. At the age of 47, Martina missed her comeback in the singles competition. Maybe she had overestimated her chances. She played this year her last singles tour in Roland-Garros. Her first appearance in the French Open dated from 1973, 31 years ago. She evens the time record of the French Andree Varin.

Martina Navratilova

Elena Dementieva

Justine Henin-Hardenne

when her sister was defeated by the winner to be Anastasia Myskina (6/3, 6/4).

"It is more than disappointment. It's frustration. Frustration because I can not control my nerves." That's the summary of Amelie Mauresmo's two weeks in Roland-Garros. The French No. 1 didn't make it pass the quarterfinals. She had to deal with too much pressure and was like paralysed. She could not play as she would have liked in front of the Russian Elena Dementieva. She lost 6/4, 6/3.

"It's difficult for me to play here. I'm French and I'm playing in France. This morning I was feeling more pressure than in other matches. The other Grand Slams are easier to manage. Maybe if I

do well there, I could find a solution to play better here and progress." Maybe. However, Amelie was quite self-confident as she had just captured two recent titles in Berlin and Rome (two Tier I). She would have liked to imitate her predecessors Steffi Graf and Monica Seles who had also captured those titles and then Roland-Garros (Graf in 1987 and Seles in 1990). The way to victory seemed however easy, even easier since Henin-Hardenne, Davenport, and the Williams sisters were not in the race anymore. But other players took advantage of it. Anastasia Myskina, for example, jumped at the opportunity.

So beating her here was good for me. Then my confidence was growing."

Justine Henin-Hardenne had forgotten her confidence in the locker room. However weakened by a viral infection similar to mononucleosis (cytomegalovirus), she came to Paris to defend her title. But the willpower was not enough. Her physical shape did match her motivation. After a tough match where she beat Sandrine Testud on the first day, she failed to advance to the third round. The Italian Tathiana Garbin ousted her in two sets (7/5, 6/4). The Belgian registered a sad record. Since 1925, only the Hungarian Zsuzsi Kormoczy, top seed No. 1 as Justine was, had been defeated in the second round. It was in 1960 against the Egyptian Betsy Abbas. Henin imitated Arantxa Sanchez-Vicario, who had also fallen in the second round in 1990, while she was defending her title.

But Justine was not the only disappointment of the week. For the first time since their first appearance together in a Grand Slam tournament (Australian Open in 1998), the two Williams sisters were eliminated on the same day, in quarterfinals. This failure resulted from a lack of preparation due to several injuries. Serena Williams does have limits. She lost to Jennifer Capriati 6/3, 2/6, 6/3,

Gaudio is the Hero of the Argentine Thriller

Roland-Garros two weeks were full of emotion, from the first match in the first round till the final match.

As from historic match between Fabrice Santoro and Arnaud Clement to the last fight between two Argentines Guillermo Coria and Gaston Gaudio. A real show!

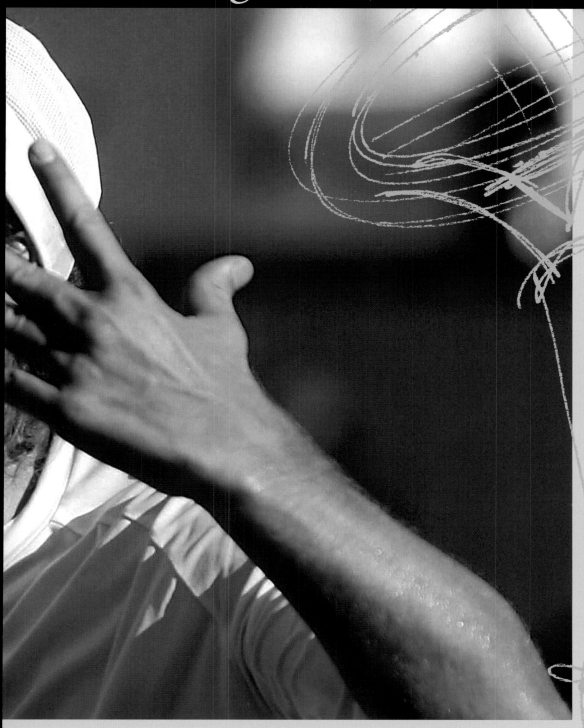

Guillermo Vilas was in the audience. No matter the match's ending, he was happy to know that another Argentine would capture the title he had taken in 1977. This Argentine's name is Gaston Gaudio, only 44th-ranked. At the age of 25, he had only two titles on his list of awards. No Grand Slam. His best performance in Roland-Garros was reached in 2002 when he was in the last sixteen. This year, he was the hero of an amazing final match against his fellow Guillermo Coria. John McEnroe said: "In the men's Race, the best match I have seen this year is the Roland-Garros final between Gaudio and Coria. At the beginning it was a one-way match, then, the audience started to support Gaudio. Gaudio was strengthened by this crowd; when he felt the audience

was with him, he relaxed and the match became completely crazy. There were Coria's cramps, a real fight till the end. We do not see very often such dramatic and crazy matches." McEnroe summed it up well. Guillermo Coria was close to victory but he failed, so Gaston Gaudio took advantage of it.

This year, an Argentine won the final. There couldn't be any other way since there were two of them in final, three in the last four. It is not a legend: Argentines do like red clay. There were four Argentines in the last eight. "Four in the quarterfinals? It is wonderful! David Nalbandian said. I am surprised, it is not normal. I would like to see four Argentines in semi-finals!" His wish almost came true. Only Juan Ignacio Chela could not do anything in front

396

Six hours and thirty-three minutes. 396 minutes. That's the time it took Fabrice Santoro to beat Arnaud Clement in 71 games in the first round. Both French men fought in this historic match that was played over two days. A record.

The historic match

First round. Fabrice Santoro defeated Arnaud Clement 6/4, 6/3, 6/7, 3/6, 16/14
Six hours and thirty-three minutes!

They are now history. Never before, a tennis match had lasted this long. Mats Wilander and John McEnroe had spent 6.22 hours on the court to finish up their quarterfinals in 1982. Fabrice Santoro and Arnaud Clement did even better or at least longer. They closed 71 games in 6.33 hours. They reached this record over two days because they had to postpone the end of the match at 5/5 in the fifth set to the next day due to sunset. The next day, after having lost a second match point, Clement left the victory to his opponent. "The record? I do not care at all", Arnaud Clement reacted. "Do I have a medal thanks to this record? No. So I am not interested in it!" We may understand his bitterness, as well as Santoro's happiness: "There is no better place to reach such a record. I am proud of myself as I gave all I had. When you want something, everything is possible."

Fabrice Santoro

of surprising Tim Henman although he usually shines on fast surface. Henman advanced to the last eight with high self-confidence, especially after his victory in the Paris-Bercy Masters Series last November. "This year, I wanted to show I am not the man of only one tournament like Wimbledon", he admitted. And he proved it! He was the first British to be in the French Open semi-finals since Mike Sangster in 1963. Three Argentines and one British in semi-finals. Nalbandian (winner over Marat Safin and Gustavo Kuerten) against Gaudio (winner over Hewitt in quarterfinals). Henman (defeated Chela and Llodra) against Coria (defeated Moya and Escude). And everybody knows how it ended.

The first week was also interesting. There were happy events and less happy events. Let us start with the American slump: no American player made it to the third round. It never happened in a Men's Grand Slam, except in the 1973 Australian Open, when no player from the United States moved to Australia. Many players made an early exit as from the second round. Like for instance Andy Roddick, ousted by Olivier Mutis (3/6, 6/3, 6/7, 6/3, 6/2). This will remain one of the best moments of the French's career. "It is the first time I do something the right way in my career", he insisted. In the second round also, the top seed No. 4 Juan Carlos Ferrero disappeared. The Spaniard did just like Justine, he stopped

Tim Henman

in the second round as a defending champ. He was ousted by Igor Andreev 6/4, 6/2, 6/3. The former world No. 1 failed to achieve his goal this season. Several injuries and chicken pox did not help. What can be said about the current world No. 1? Roger Federer was defeated in the third round by the three-time winner Gustavo Kuerten 6/4, 6/4, 6/4. But the worse confrontation came from a young Frenchman. No

sense of values anymore. No respect for the oldest. As from the first day, Jerome Haenel defeated Andre Agassi in three short sets 6/4, 7/6, 6/3. He was then 271st-ranked and beat his hero, former world No. 1 and former champion (in 1999). The 23-year-old man captured his first match on the main Race. He was almost as happy as if he had earned the title, almost as happy as Gaston Gaudio.

Guillermo Coria

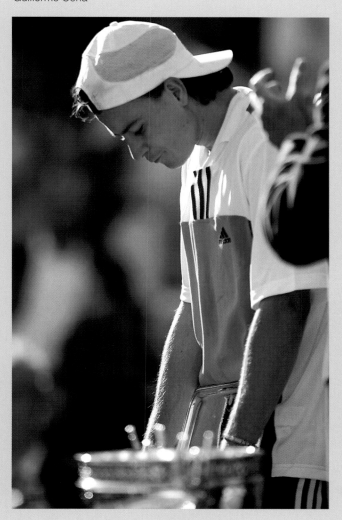

Final's Screenplay

Gaston Gaudio Defeated Guillermo Coria 0/6, 3/6, 6/4, 6/1, 8/6

It happened on Sunday June 6, 2004, on a sunny afternoon. Both players went through different moods: from shame to confidence, from assurance to perdition, from joy to sadness, from distress to euphoria, from abasement to compassion, from stress to relaxation. Gaston Gaudio lost the first set 6/0. Hard for him. He didn't wake up in the second set. The audience was almost sorry to attend such a terrible meeting. After one hour, it seemed to be it for Coria. The latter won the second set rather easily. Gaudio was nervous and it is understandable. Especially the audience understood. Spurred on by the loud Parisian crowd on the Court Central, the poor Gaston started to relax. It loosened him up. After all, he was in the Roland-Garros final match, which is not bad at all, no matter what the result of this match is. He started waking up. He was obviously happy. After having thanked the audience with applause, he came back into the game little by little. He snatched the third set. This was when the situation was reversed. Coria fell. He was paralysed by cramping legs. The physiotherapist came but Coria had to wait, wait and play. But he could hardly run. He could not serve normally. "I was rather thinking about cramps than the match. They told me I had to wait about 10 minutes after the cream, and after that I would be able to move more", he explained. While he was waiting for his cramps to disappear, Gaudio tried to catch up with the score. At the end of the fifth set, Coria had two match points, at 5/4, and then at 6/5. But the 44th-ranked Gaudio saved them and ended up lifting the French Open trophy after 3.30 hours of sensational match. Gaston then thanked the audience, his audience. Like a football player after victory, he ran around the court to greet his fans. Just to make sure that it was not a dream.

ROLAND-GARROS

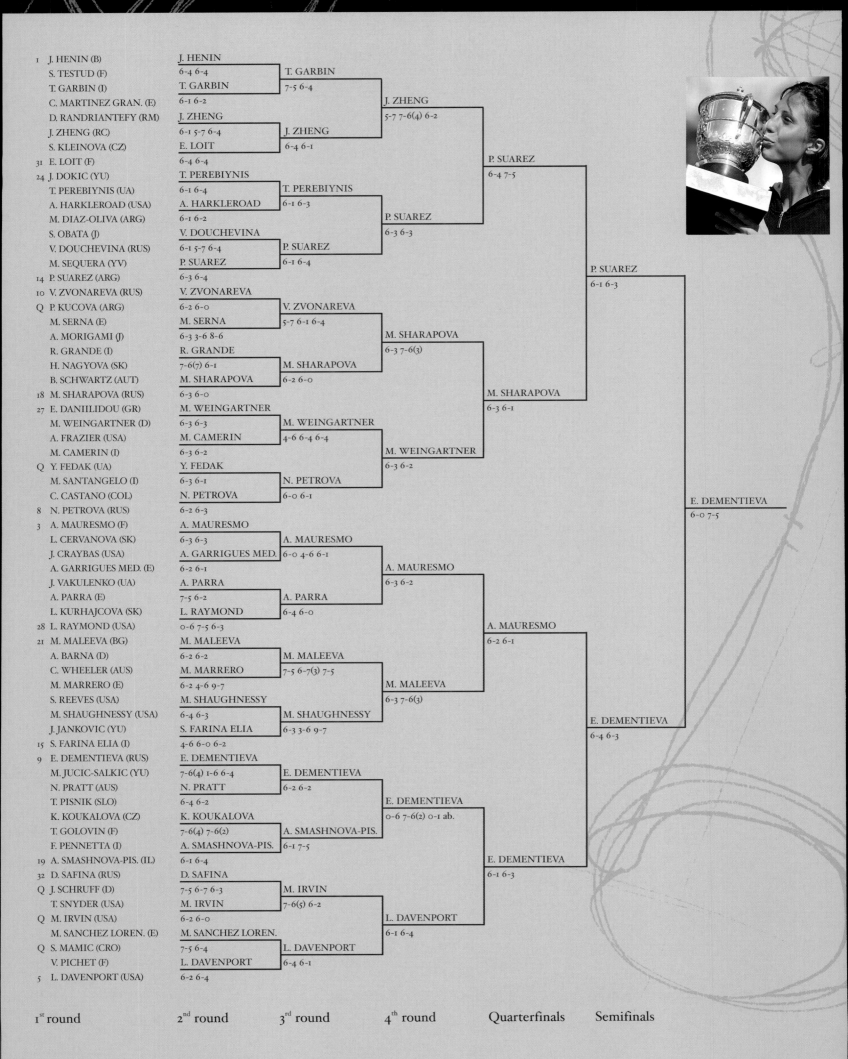

| 1st round | 2nd round | 3rd round | 4th round | Quarterfinals | Semifinals |

1st round players and seeds:

1 J. HENIN (B)
S. TESTUD (F)
T. GARBIN (I)
C. MARTINEZ GRAN. (E)
D. RANDRIANTEFY (RM)
J. ZHENG (RC)
S. KLEINOVA (CZ)
31 E. LOIT (F)
24 J. DOKIC (YU)
T. PEREBIYNIS (UA)
A. HARKLEROAD (USA)
M. DIAZ-OLIVA (ARG)
S. OBATA (J)
V. DOUCHEVINA (RUS)
M. SEQUERA (YV)
14 P. SUAREZ (ARG)
10 V. ZVONAREVA (RUS)
Q P. KUCOVA (ARG)
M. SERNA (E)
A. MORIGAMI (J)
R. GRANDE (I)
H. NAGYOVA (SK)
B. SCHWARTZ (AUT)
18 M. SHARAPOVA (RUS)
27 E. DANIILIDOU (GR)
M. WEINGARTNER (D)
A. FRAZIER (USA)
M. CAMERIN (I)
Q Y. FEDAK (UA)
M. SANTANGELO (I)
C. CASTANO (COL)
8 N. PETROVA (RUS)
3 A. MAURESMO (F)
L. CERVANOVA (SK)
J. CRAYBAS (USA)
A. GARRIGUES MED. (E)
J. VAKULENKO (UA)
A. PARRA (E)
L. KURHAJCOVA (SK)
28 L. RAYMOND (USA)
21 M. MALEEVA (BG)
A. BARNA (D)
C. WHEELER (AUS)
M. MARRERO (E)
S. REEVES (USA)
M. SHAUGHNESSY (USA)
J. JANKOVIC (YU)
15 S. FARINA ELIA (I)
9 E. DEMENTIEVA (RUS)
M. JUCIC-SALKIC (YU)
N. PRATT (AUS)
T. PISNIK (SLO)
K. KOUKALOVA (CZ)
T. GOLOVIN (F)
F. PENNETTA (I)
19 A. SMASHNOVA-PIS. (IL)
32 D. SAFINA (RUS)
Q J. SCHRUFF (D)
T. SNYDER (USA)
Q M. IRVIN (USA)
M. SANCHEZ LOREN. (E)
Q S. MAMIC (CRO)
V. PICHET (F)
5 L. DAVENPORT (USA)

2nd round:

J. HENIN 6-4 6-4
T. GARBIN 6-1 6-2
J. ZHENG 6-1 5-7 6-4
E. LOIT 6-4 6-4
T. PEREBIYNIS 6-1 6-4
A. HARKLEROAD 6-1 6-2
V. DOUCHEVINA 6-1 5-7 6-4
P. SUAREZ 6-3 6-4
V. ZVONAREVA 6-2 6-0
M. SERNA 6-3 3-6 8-6
R. GRANDE 7-6(7) 6-1
M. SHARAPOVA 6-3 6-0
M. WEINGARTNER 6-3 6-3
M. CAMERIN 6-3 6-2
Y. FEDAK 6-3 6-1
N. PETROVA 6-2 6-3
A. MAURESMO 6-3 6-3
A. GARRIGUES MED. 6-2 6-1
A. PARRA 7-5 6-2
L. RAYMOND 0-6 7-5 6-3
M. MALEEVA 6-2 6-2
M. MARRERO 6-2 4-6 9-7
M. SHAUGHNESSY 6-4 6-3
S. FARINA ELIA 4-6 6-0 6-2
E. DEMENTIEVA 7-6(4) 1-6 6-4
N. PRATT 6-4 6-2
K. KOUKALOVA 7-6(4) 7-6(2)
A. SMASHNOVA-PIS. 6-1 6-4
D. SAFINA 7-5 6-7 6-3
M. IRVIN 6-2 6-0
M. SANCHEZ LOREN. 7-5 6-4
L. DAVENPORT 6-2 6-4

3rd round:

T. GARBIN 7-5 6-4
J. ZHENG 6-4 6-1
T. PEREBIYNIS 6-1 6-3
P. SUAREZ 6-1 6-4
V. ZVONAREVA 5-7 6-1 6-4
M. SHARAPOVA 6-2 6-0
M. WEINGARTNER 4-6 6-4 6-4
N. PETROVA 6-0 6-1
A. MAURESMO 6-0 4-6 6-1
A. PARRA 6-4 6-0
M. MALEEVA 7-5 6-7(3) 7-5
M. SHAUGHNESSY 6-3 3-6 9-7
E. DEMENTIEVA 6-2 6-2
A. SMASHNOVA-PIS. 6-1 7-5
M. IRVIN 7-6(5) 6-2
L. DAVENPORT 6-4 6-1

4th round:

J. ZHENG 5-7 7-6(4) 6-2
P. SUAREZ 6-3 6-3
M. SHARAPOVA 6-3 7-6(3)
M. WEINGARTNER 6-3 6-2
A. MAURESMO 6-3 6-2
M. MALEEVA 6-3 7-6(3)
E. DEMENTIEVA 0-6 7-6(2) 0-1 ab.
L. DAVENPORT 6-1 6-4

Quarterfinals:

P. SUAREZ 6-4 7-5
M. SHARAPOVA 6-3 6-1
A. MAURESMO 6-2 6-1
E. DEMENTIEVA 6-1 6-3

Semifinals:

P. SUAREZ 6-1 6-3
E. DEMENTIEVA 6-4 6-3

Final:

E. DEMENTIEVA 6-0 7-5

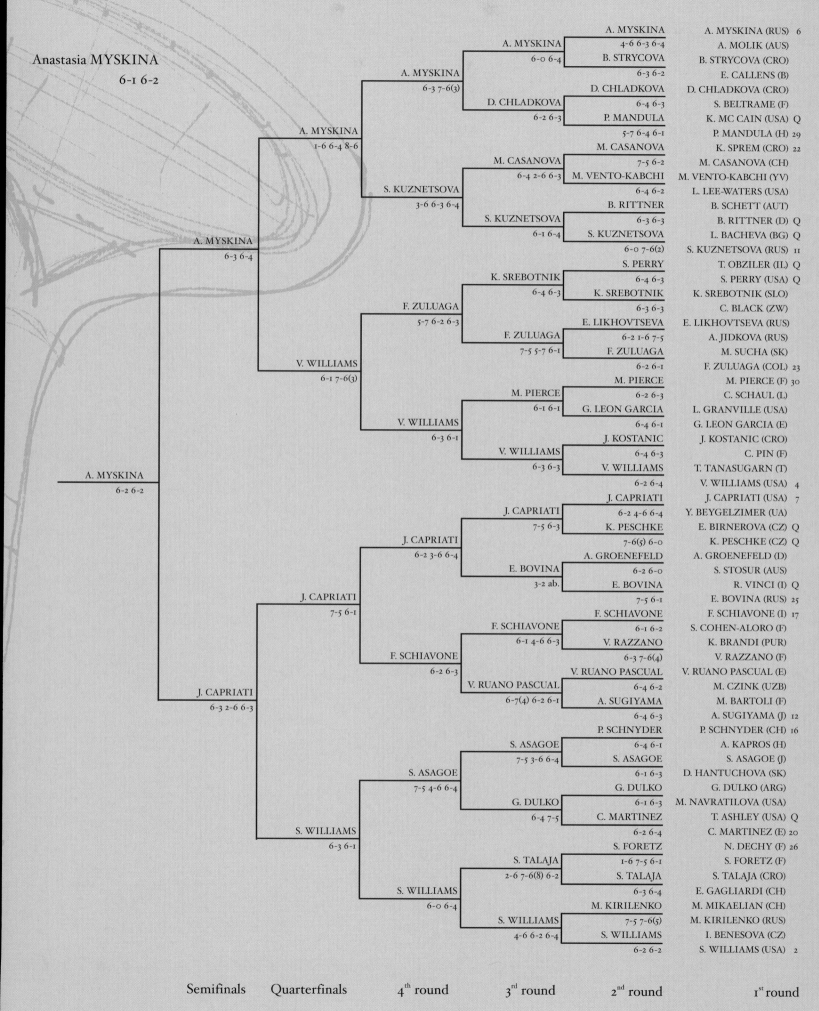

Anastasia MYSKINA
6-1 6-2

| Semifinals | Quarterfinals | 4th round | 3rd round | 2nd round | 1st round |

ROLAND-GARROS

1st round

1 R. FEDERER (CH)
Q K. VLIEGEN (B)
T. ASCIONE (F)
N. KIEFER (D)
R. RAMIREZ HIDAL. (E)
G. ELSENEER (B)
Q N. ALMAGRO (E)
28 G. KUERTEN (BR)
23 F. LOPEZ (E)
N. LAPENTTI (EC)
I. KARLOVIC (CRO)
K. KUCERA (SK)
O. PATIENCE (F)
F. VOLANDRI (I)
R. SODERLING (S)
Q H. LEE (KOR)
10 S. GROSJEAN (F)
Q K. KIM (USA)
Q P. STARACE (I)
D. TURSUNOV (RUS)
F. MANTILLA (E)
Q J. SALZENSTEIN (USA)
A. CALLERI (ARG)
20 M. SAFIN (RUS)
25 I. LJUBICIC (CRO)
H. ARAZI (MA)
S. KOUBEK (A)
D. SANCHEZ (E)
K. PLESS (DK)
Q A. FALLA (COL)
R. GASQUET (F)
8 D. NALBANDIAN (ARG)
4 J. FERRERO (E)
T. HAAS (D)
J. VACEK (CZ)
I. ANDREEV (RUS)
O. ROCHUS (B)
D. FERRER (E)
J. BENNETEAU (F)
29 M. MIRNYI (BG)
24 J. BJORKMAN (S)
T. DENT (USA)
K. CARLSEN (DK)
T. ENQVIST (S)
G. CANAS (ARG)
G. GAUDIO (ARG)
A. DUPUIS (F)
14 J. NOVAK (CZ)
12 L. HEWITT (AUS)
A. DI PASQUALE (F)
J. MELZER (AUT)
W. FERREIRA (AFS)
V. HANESCU (RU)
J. LISNARD (F)
J. BOUTTER (F)
19 M. VERKERK (NL)
26 A. COSTA (E)
F. SARETTA (BR)
C. ROCHUS (B)
Q M. LOPEZ (E)
Q D. ELSNER (D)
Q A. PEYA (AUT)
X. MALISSE (B)
7 R. SCHUETTLER (D)

2nd round

R. FEDERER — 6-1 6-2 6-1
N. KIEFER — 6-3 6-2 6-2
G. ELSENEER — 3-6 7-5 4-6 6-4 6-3
G. KUERTEN — 7-5 7-6(2) 1-6 3-6 7-5
F. LOPEZ — 5-7 6-4 6-4 6-4
K. KUCERA — 7-6(4) 6-4 6-4
O. PATIENCE — 6-3 7-6(5) 6-0
H. LEE — 0-6 3-6 6-3 6-4 7-5
S. GROSJEAN — 6-1 6-1 6-4
P. STARACE — 6-2 6-3 6-4
F. MANTILLA — 6-4 6-1 6-7(6) 6-2
M. SAFIN — 5-7 6-1 4-1 ab.
I. LJUBICIC — 6-7(3) 6-4 6-7(2) 6-3 6-3
S. KOUBEK — 6-3 7-5 3-6 6-7(0) 6-0
A. FALLA — 6-2 4-6 6-1 6-2
D. NALBANDIAN — 6-4 7-5 7-6(1)
J. FERRERO — 3-6 6-4 6-4 6-2
I. ANDREEV — 6-3 6-1 6-4
D. FERRER — 6-1 6-1 6-3
J. BENNETEAU — 7-5 7-5 1-6 6-3
J. BJORKMAN — 6-3 2-6 6-3 3-6 6-2
T. ENQVIST — 6-2 6-3 6-4
G. GAUDIO — 6-2 2-6 4-6 6-3 6-2
J. NOVAK — 6-4 6-4 6-7(4) 6-3
L. HEWITT — 6-0 7-6(5) 4-6 6-1
J. MELZER — 6-7(4) 6-2 6-4 6-3
V. HANESCU — 7-5 6-2 6-4
M. VERKERK — 7-5 6-3 6-1
A. COSTA — 6-2 6-2 6-7(2) 6-4
C. ROCHUS — 6-4 6-1 6-1
D. ELSNER — 6-1 7-6(4) 6-2
X. MALISSE — 6-3 4-0 ab.

3rd round

R. FEDERER — 6-3 6-4 7-6(6)
G. KUERTEN — 6-2 6-0 6-3
F. LOPEZ — 6-7(3) 6-3 6-4 6-4
H. LEE — 6-4 6-4 6-3
P. STARACE — 7-6(6) 6-3 6-4
M. SAFIN — 6-4 2-6 6-2 6-7(4) 11-9
S. KOUBEK — 6-0 1-6 6-4 6-2
D. NALBANDIAN — 5-7 6-0 6-2 6-0
I. ANDREEV — 6-4 6-2 6-3
J. BENNETEAU — 6-3 1-6 6-2 7-5
T. ENQVIST — 6-3 3-6 7-6(8) 6-3
G. GAUDIO — 2-6 6-4 6-4 5-7 6-3
L. HEWITT — 6-4 6-4 4-6 6-2
M. VERKERK — 4-6 6-3 3-6 6-0 3-0 ab.
A. COSTA — 6-1 6-2 7-5
X. MALISSE — 6-4 7-5 6-4

4th round

G. KUERTEN — 6-4 6-4 6-4
F. LOPEZ — 7-6(3) 4-6 6-0 6-3
M. SAFIN — 6-7(4) 6-4 3-6 7-5 7-5
D. NALBANDIAN — 6-7(1) 6-3 7-6(1) 7-5
I. ANDREEV — 7-6(3) 7-6(3) 6-3
G. GAUDIO — 6-0 6-4 6-7(5) 6-4
L. HEWITT — 6-2 3-6 4-6 6-2 6-1
X. MALISSE — 6-4 2-6 4-6 7-6(4) 8-6

Quarterfinals

G. KUERTEN — 6-3 7-5 6-4
D. NALBANDIAN — 7-5 6-4 6-7(5) 6-3
G. GAUDIO — 6-4 7-5 6-3
L. HEWITT — 7-5 6-2 7-6(6)

Semifinals

D. NALBANDIAN — 6-2 3-6 6-4 7-6(6)
G. GAUDIO — 6-3 6-2 6-2

Final

G. GAUDIO — 6-3 7-6(5) 6-0

1st round   2nd round   3rd round   4th round   Quarterfinals   Semifinals

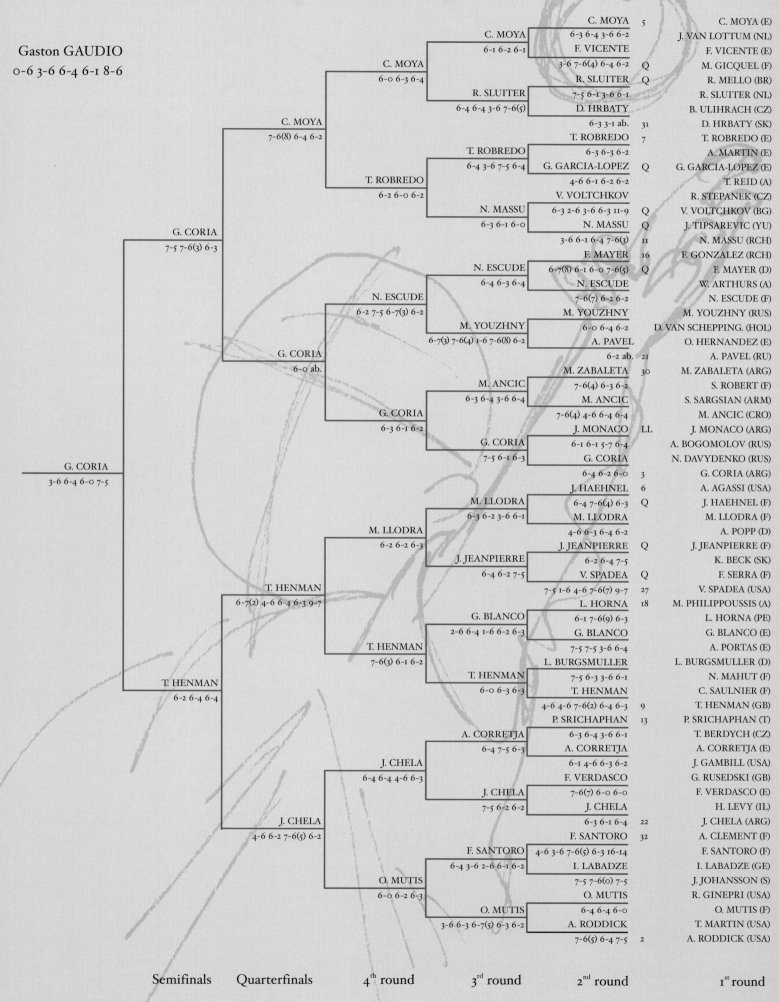

Gaston GAUDIO

0-6 3-6 6-4 6-1 8-6

Semifinals   Quarterfinals   4ᵗʰ round   3ʳᵈ round   2ⁿᵈ round   1ˢᵗ round

*walkover

ROLAND-GARROS

The finalists (statistics dated from 07.06.2004)

Anastasia Myskina

Russia
Bithdate: July 08, 1981
Birthplace: Moscow, Russia
Height: 5'8 1/2"
Weight: 130 1/2 lbs.
Plays: Right-handed
List of Awards: 8 titles, including one Grand Slam
(Roland-Garros 2004)

Elena Dementieva

Russia
Birthdate: October 15, 1981
Birthplace: Moscow, Russia
Height: 5'11"
Weight: 141 lbs.
Plays: Right-handed
List of Awards: 3 titles (no Grand Slam)

Gaston Gaudio

Argentine
Birthdate: December 09, 1978
Birthplace: Buenos Aires, Argentine
Height: 5'9"
Weight: 155 lbs.
Plays: Right-handed
Pro since: 1996
List of awards: 3 titles, including 1 Grand Slam
(Roland-Garros 2004)

Guillermo Coria

Argentine
Birthdate: January 13, 1982
Birthplace: Rufino, Argentine
Height: 5'10"
Weight: 150 lbs.
Plays: Right-handed
Pro since: 2000
List of Awards: 8 titles (no Grand Slam)

Olivier Rochus and Xavier Malisse

The girls

Sesil Karatancheva Got It!
She was the favourite. Training at the Nick Bollettieri academy, the Bulgarian Sesil Karatancheva is only 14. She is the third Russian girl to lift the Roland-Garros Girls Trophy, after Manuela Maleeva in 1982 and Magdanela Maleeva in 1990. She did not drop any set during the tour. In final, she easily defeated Madalina Gojnea 6/4, 6/0.

The Boys

Monfils, French Hope
Already winner at the Australian Open in the beginning of the year (victory against his mate Josselin Ouanna), Gael Monfils managed his stress like a master in final against the American Kuznetsov (6/2, 6/2). Gaël was flying over the tournament. He lost only one set in six matches (in the first round against the Spanish Guillermo Alcaide-Justell). And to finish on a nice point, he closed the final match with an ace on his second serve. The last French who had won boys' Roland-Garros was Richard Gasquet (2002). In total, twelve French boys have captured this title. With two consecutive Grand Slam titles, Monfils is getting closer and closer to the world No. 1 rank in the Boys' category.

Women's doubles

And that's three!

"We did not think we could win so easily, Virginia Ruano Pascual said. To reach final for the ninth consecutive time and to be in Roland-Garros' final for the third time, I am really proud of it!" Paola Suarez is also very proud of it: "I think the other players do not like to play us because we do not have a common game. It is very reassuring to feel they know it will be hard to play us." Indeed, the Russian pair Kuznetsova/Likhovtseva had a hard time in the final match against the Spanish-Argentine pair, who captured their third consecutive Grand Slam title. Virginia and Paola added a sixth Grand Slam to their list of awards, the third one in Roland-Garros (after their victories of 2001 and 2002).

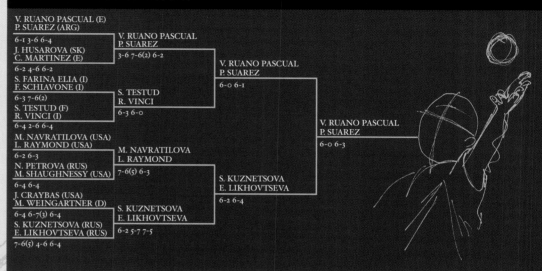

Women's Doubles Results

V. RUANO PASCUAL (E)
P. SUAREZ (ARG)
6-1 3-6 6-4
— V. RUANO PASCUAL / P. SUAREZ
J. HUSAROVA (SK)
C. MARTINEZ (E)
6-2 4-6 6-2
3-6 7-6(2) 6-2
— V. RUANO PASCUAL / P. SUAREZ
6-0 6-1

S. FARINA ELIA (I)
F. SCHIAVONE (I)
6-3 7-6(2)
— S. TESTUD / R. VINCI
S. TESTUD (F)
R. VINCI (I)
6-4 2-6 6-4
6-3 6-0

— V. RUANO PASCUAL / P. SUAREZ
6-0 6-3

M. NAVRATILOVA (USA)
L. RAYMOND (USA)
6-2 6-3
— M. NAVRATILOVA / L. RAYMOND
N. PETROVA (RUS)
M. SHAUGHNESSY (USA)
6-4 6-4
7-6(5) 6-3

— S. KUZNETSOVA / E. LIKHOVTSEVA
6-2 6-4

J. CRAYBAS (USA)
M. WEINGARTNER (D)
6-4 6-7(3) 6-4
— S. KUZNETSOVA / E. LIKHOVTSEVA
S. KUZNETSOVA (RUS)
E. LIKHOVTSEVA (RUS)
7-6(5) 4-6 6-4
6-2 5-7 7-5

Mixed doubles

Golovin and Gasquet Just For Fun!

"It is just great because in the beginning, we did it just for fun, we did not expect to win. And eventually it is a great victory." Both of them were defeated in the first singles round, so Tatiana Golovin and Richard Gasquet decided to play together in the mixed doubles. Just to have some fun. The youngest team of the tournament brilliantly dominated top seeds No. 2 Virginia Ruano Pascual and Marl Knowles and finally the Zimbabwean pair Cara and Wayne Black. Thirty-one years after Françoise Dürr and Jean-Claude Barclay, another French pair won a mixed doubles. "You do not capture a Grand Slam title every day!" Golovin admitted. And she added: "Next year, we will win the singles final!"

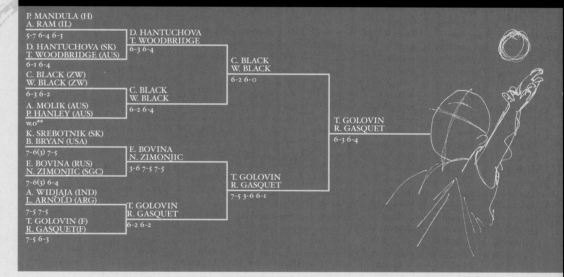

Mixed Doubles Results

P. MANDULA (H)
A. RAM (IL)
5-7 6-4 6-3
— D. HANTUCHOVA / T. WOODBRIDGE
D. HANTUCHOVA (SK)
T. WOODBRIDGE (AUS)
6-1 6-4
6-3 6-4

— C. BLACK / W. BLACK
6-2 6-0

C. BLACK (ZW)
W. BLACK (ZW)
6-3 6-2
— C. BLACK / W. BLACK
A. MOLIK (AUS)
P. HANLEY (AUS)
w.o**
6-2 6-4

— T. GOLOVIN / R. GASQUET
6-3 6-4

K. SREBOTNIK (SK)
B. BRYAN (USA)
7-6(3) 7-5
— E. BOVINA / N. ZIMONJIC
E. BOVINA (RUS)
N. ZIMONJIC (SGC)
7-6(3) 6-4
3-6 7-5 7-5

— T. GOLOVIN / R. GASQUET
7-5 3-6 6-1

A. WIDJAJA (IND)
L. ARNOLD (ARG)
7-5 7-5
— T. GOLOVIN / R. GASQUET
T. GOLOVIN (F)
R. GASQUET (F)
7-5 6-3
6-2 6-2

Men's doubles

Self-confident Rochus and Malisse

Like in 2003, there were two Belgians in a final match in Roland-Garros. The men's doubles final match. Olivier Rochus and Xavier Malisse played against the French Fabrice Santoro and Michael Llodra. The French thought they were through with the toughest when they ousted seeds No. 4 Knowles/Nestor in quarterfinals and Bryan brothers, top seeds No. 1 and defending champions. They were the favourites in front of this Belgian pair (neither Malisse nor Rochus had reached a doubles final before), who defeated five top seeds in six rounds. But Santoro could still feel the 6.33 long hours of play against Arnaud Clement in the singles match. He paid for it today and the price was high as they were defeated in two sets 7/5, 7/5.

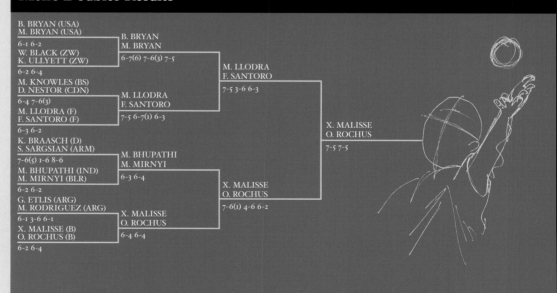

Men's Doubles Results

B. BRYAN (USA)
M. BRYAN (USA)
6-1 6-2
— B. BRYAN / M. BRYAN
W. BLACK (ZW)
K. ULLYETT (ZW)
6-2 6-4
6-7(6) 7-6(3) 7-5

— M. LLODRA / F. SANTORO
7-5 3-6 6-3

M. KNOWLES (BS)
D. NESTOR (CDN)
6-4 7-6(3)
— M. LLODRA / F. SANTORO
M. LLODRA (F)
F. SANTORO (F)
6-3 6-2
7-5 6-7(1) 6-3

— X. MALISSE / O. ROCHUS
7-5 7-5

K. BRAASCH (D)
S. SARGSIAN (ARM)
7-6(5) 1-6 8-6
— M. BHUPATHI / M. MIRNYI
M. BHUPATHI (IND)
M. MIRNYI (BLR)
6-2 6-2
6-3 6-4

— X. MALISSE / O. ROCHUS
7-6(1) 4-6 6-2

G. ETLIS (ARG)
M. RODRIGUEZ (ARG)
6-1 3-6 6-1
— X. MALISSE / O. ROCHUS
X. MALISSE (B)
O. ROCHUS (B)
6-2 6-4
6-4 6-4

* walkover

Russian Invasion

This year, three Grand Slams out of four have been captured by Russians. Three girls: Anastasia Myskina at Roland-Garros, Maria Sharapova at Wimbledon and Svetlana Kuznetsova at the US Open. Quite a revolution in women's tennis history.

" I do not think that 2004 was the year of the maturation but well the year of the awareness "

Olga Morozova,
Elena Dementieva's coach

Anastasia Myskina, Maria Sharapova, Svetlana Kuznetsova

I was talking about it with Vera Zvonareva, who was then world No. 12 and told me: I am the No. 6 in Russia, meaning I am almost nothing."

Nadia Petrova, world No. 12 in 2003, has a clear point of view on the situation: "After the Perestroika, everything was found to be possible. People realised they could make money with sport. Then they started to train seriously not only thinking of having fun but also thinking it was their job. The first to do so was Anna Kournikova. After her, many came along. Our first quality is our physical strength, we are very strong." So they all owe part of their success to Anna Kournikova. The latter is still drawing the attention of the media, appearing in all sorts of magazines or fashion shows but she is also laughed at in the tennis field for her short list of awards. However, she showed her countrywomen it was possible to defeat the world's best players. Her semi-final match in Wimbledon in 1997, when she was only 16, reassured many of them. Kournikova nonetheless reached the world's first rank in doubles draw and the eighth in singles.

It was in 2000 that Elena Dementieva followed her steps with a semi-final match at the US Open and a gold medal at the Olympic Games in Sydney. But no major WTA title yet. As time goes by, more and more Russian players take part in tournaments. Dementieva eventually captured her first title in 2003 in Amelia Island. A little later, there was a strong 'Slavian atmosphere' at Roland-Garros. Nadia Petrova ousted Monica Seles and Jennifer Capriati, and sailed to semi-finals. As for Vera Zvonareva, she defeated Venus Williams before losing against Petrova in quarterfinals. The same year, Svetlana Kuznetsova reached quarterfinals in Wimbledon after defeating the wild-card Maria Sharapova. At the US Open, Myskina reached the quarterfinals. Dementieva captured Bali and Shangai tournaments and joined Myskina in the top 10. Nothing could stop them. In 2004, they were at the top of the three most expected events of the year. After the Moscow Open, Russia held an amount of nine titles since January 1 (including the three Grand Slams). "I do not think that 2004 was the year of the maturation but well the year of the awareness," Olga Morozova (Elena Dementieva's coach) stated. "Tennis is a question of faith. When they see one of them defeating Davenport, another one beating Mauresmo, they think: 'Why not me? I train as much as the others, there is no reason that it does not work!' Then, it is the usual process: victory comes with confidence."

Last June, on Roland-Garros last day, Chamil Tarpichev gave some advice: "Today's result is not a chance but the consequence of long hours of hard work. We have the means to go on progressing. A lot of little girls will also start to dream." If so, Russians will still be fearful opponents for everyone in 2005 and for more years to come. Kim, Justine, Serena and the others have to be careful. A lot of -ova family names are hiding great champions.

Justine, Kim and Serena have been in the spotlight only because they were out of the courts for a long time. Maybe, if they had not been injured, the situation would have been different. It is even more than certain. However, if Myskina, Sharapova, Kuznetsova and even Dementieva (twice a Grand Slam finalist this year) marked the 2004 season, it is also thanks to the way they played tennis: Anastasia in Roland-Garros, Maria in Wimbledon and Svetlana in Flushing Meadows. Those are the names of three Russian girls who excelled on three different surfaces. The President of the Russian federation, Shamil Tarpischev, had stated at the end of 2002: "Within a few years, our nation will be dominating in tennis, especially in the women's Tour." He probably did not think he would be so right and that it would come this quick. The girls followed Evgueni Kafelnikov and Marat Safin's examples (three Grand Slams titles together and fifteen weeks as world No. 1). This year, there were sometimes five of them in the world top 10. Only the United States had reached such a performance.

Russian women's tennis level is much higher than the men's. In 2002, there were eight of them in the world top 100, none of them in the top 10. Today there are fifteen in the top 100 (twice as many). The Russians have been invading the world top ranking. There are so many of them now that they have to compete against each other. "There is such a competition between the Russian players," Svetlana Kuznetsova explained. "All of us want to be national No. 1 in Russia. Not so long ago

Anastasia MYSKINA
(Statistics dated from October 18, 2004)

Birth date: July 8, 1981
Birthplace: Moscow, Russia
Height: 5'8 1/2"
Weight: 130 1/2 lbs.
Pro since: 1999
Best ranking: No. 2 (September 13, 2004)
WTA Tour titles: 9 singles

2004	Doha, Roland-Garros, Moscow
2003	Doha, Sarasota, Leipzig, Moscow
2002	Bahia
1999	Palermo

The First of All

Anastasia Myskina, (Roland-Garros winner)

The first Russian major title. Anastasia Myskina may be honoured for being the first Russian woman to capture a Grand Slam title. This happened this year in Roland-Garros. But it could also have been the other finalist Elena Dementieva who got it. The first ever all-Russian final. Anastasia opened the 2004 happy events. She showed her countrywomen it is possible to win. Anastasia Myskina started to play tennis at the age of six years old at Spartak Moscow, together with a girl called Elena Dementieva. Their first coach was Rosa Islanova, Marat and Dinara Safin's mother. The strict woman taught them the basic skills for about ten years. In 1999, Anastasia captured her first title in Palermo under Sviatoslav Mirza's coaching. At that time, her father, who was working as a policeman, decided to take care of her fulltime. "If she wants to be a champion, there is only one thing to do: work hard." Myskina worked hard for three years before meeting Jens Gerlach, both coach and lover at the end of 2002. He provided her with the confidence she needed. Her father was putting her under too much pressure. And then, she started to capture several victories until this historic day in Russian women tennis: Saturday June 5, 2004. That happened in the French capital.

> " It is more important for Anastasia Myskina to be Russian No. 1 than world No. 1. But very soon, to remain Russian No. 1, she will have no other choice to capture the world first rank. "
>
> *Jens Gerlach,*
> *Anastasia Myskina's coach*

The Bad Comparison with Anna Kournikova

Maria Sharapova, (Wimbledon winner)

A model herself. Maria managed very quickly to prove wrong those who were seeing her as the second Anna Kournikova. However, she was first looked at for her nice look. The comparison with Anna was easy. Moreover, Maria let a high-pitched sound out each time she hit the ball. Then, she was compared to Monica Seles. Maria got fed up with all those comparisons. Maria wanted to be recognised for her game, her performances. So much the better as Maria does not fear victory. And she proved it with a surprising victory in Wimbledon, the fourth title in her career, the most important. "I am not another Anna but the first Maria. In any case, confusion is impossible: I have already won three tournaments", she said after her title in Birmingham. In the eighties, the Sharapov family was living in Gomel, near Tchernobyl. The mother was pregnant during the nuclear explosion so they decided to move. Maria was born in Nyagan in Siberia on April 19, 1987. At the age of four, she discovered tennis, encouraged by her father, a driver. One day, they went to Moscow and met Martina Navratilova, who was impressed by little Masha's talent: "Go to Nick Bollettieri in Florida! They will give her forehand and backhand. They hit millions of balls there." The piece of advice was followed immediately: Maria and her father were convinced that her future tennis career would be built in the United States. At seven years old, she arrived in Florida with Yuri (but without her mother, who could not obtain a visa) and she earned a scholarship to study at the Nick Bollettieri Academy. Her father, who arrived with only US$ 700, found different jobs to support his daughter. "I was in a room with 16-year-old girls, who were not very nice to me", Maria summed up. "For two years, I have not seen my mother, who could not come to see us in the USA. I learned to fight." A few years later, Maria indeed fought hard to defeat former world No. 1 Serena Williams in the final at Wimbledon. She was only seventeen years old. After the match, the American did not fail to congratulate her opponent: "Her victory is nice and it is interesting to see that apart from Kim (Clijsters), Justine (Henin-Hardenne), my sister (Venus) and me, another great champion is born." She's a real fighter.

"To become the best player in the world is my life's motive," Maria Sharapova concluded.

Maria SHARAPOVA
(Statistics dated from October 18, 2004)

Birth date: April 19, 1987
Birthplace: Nyagan, Russia (Siberian region)
Height: 6'
Weight: 130 lbs.
Pro since: 2001
Best ranking: 7 (August 23, 2004)
List of Awards: 6 singles

2004	Birmingham, Wimbledon, Seoul, Tokyo
2003	Tokyo [Japan Open], Quebec City

"
I wanted to win all Grand Slams titles. But now that I won Wimbledon, my next goal is to be world No. 1.
"

Maria Sharapova

Svetlana KUZNETSOVA
(Statistics dated from October 18, 2004)

Birthdate: June 27, 1985
Birthplace: St. Petersburg, Russia
Height: 5'8 1/2"
Weight: 161 lbs.
Pro since: 1999
Best ranking: 4 (October 18, 2004)
List of awards: 5 singles

2004	Eastbourne, US Open, Bali
2002	Helsinki, Bali

She Shines in Singles and Doubles

Svetlana Kuznetsova,
(2004 US Open winner)

It was expected. It was in the book. Svetlana Kuznetsova was to join the world best players. On March 5, 2004 she surprised everybody when she beat the world No. 1 Justine Henin-Hardenne at semi-finals in Doha. That was her first victory in five matches against the Belgian. A kind of a trigger: "This victory made me confident", she admitted. When you once beat the world No. 1, if you maintain your level and work hard, you can do it again. You have to believe in yourself." Svetlana has been maintaining her level, working hard, and believing in herself, again and again. It worked! A few months later, she captured the US Open. Born in a sport-like family (track cycling), Svetlana was planned to be a high-standard sportswoman. At the age of 14, she went to live in Spain to enter the Academy of Emilio Sanchez and Sergio Casal. She has the support of Arantxa Sanchez, Emilio's sister, with whom she often played in doubles tournaments, as well as of Martina Navratilova, who has been believing in her for a long time (she holds in total ten doubles titles). And when she won her US Open final, Svetlana went to Martina to cry her happiness. Given the two champs' lists of awards, Svetlana was right to follow their advice.

> " All of us want to be national No. 1 in Russia. Not so long ago I was talking about it with Vera Zvonareva, who was then world No. 12 and told me: I am the No. 6 in Russia, meaning I am almost nothing. "

Svetlana Kuznetsova

The Most Discreet of All

Elena Dementieva, (Finalist at Roland-Garros and at the US Open in 2004)

Elena Dementieva did not win a Grand title. At the age of 23, she actually did not win many titles in general. However, she was found to be in two Grand Slams finals (Roland-Garros and the US Open), which is not so bad. Coached by Olga Morozova, finalist in Roland-Garros in 1974, she is far from the star-system, in which girls like Anna Kournikova or Maria Sharapova entered easily. She doesn't go anywhere without her mother and prefers to stay far from the media as much as possible. She does not want to be in the spotlights, she want to focus on her game, on her career. It was in 2000 that people started to talk about Elena and the semi-final match she played at the US Open or her gold medal at the Olympic Games in Sydney. But no WTA Tour major title yet. But it would come sooner or later because, like her fellow countrywomen, she has got the spirit of fighter. Technically, her powerful forehand compensates for her serve, especially her second serve, which puts her into troubles. She admitted: "I know my serve's weakness. I work hard on it with Olga Morozova, my coach since last year. We already changed a lot of things, in the movement and in the shot, but I still cannot perform what I do in training in the matches. I know it will take time but I will go on working. It is clear that I won't be able to be world No. 1 or to win a Grand Slam title with such a bad serve." So Elena tried to reassure herself: "But a champion's spirit is not to be measured according to the serve's quality but rather to ambition and heart working." She is not wrong.

Elena DEMENTIEVA
(Statistics dated from October 18, 2004)

Birth date: October 15, 1981
Birthplace: Moscow, Russia
Height: 5'11"
Weight: 141 lbs.
Pro since: 1998
Best ranking: 5 (September 13, 2004)
List of awards: 4 singles

2004	Hasselt
2003	Amelia Island, Bali, Shanghai

" My coach (Olga Morozova) did not believe I could reach this level with such a bad serve. "

Elena Dementieva

The New Tsarina

At 17 years old, Maria Sharapova made a startling impression on the London grass. Sharapova looks a lot like Kournikova, but she has a little something her compatriot doesn't have, she wins. She won her first Grand Slam title thanks to a victory over the defending champion Serena Williams.

At Roland-Garros, Anastasia Myskina had the honour to become the first Russian woman to win a Grand Slam title. This performance gave bright ideas to some of her fellow countrywomen. Indeed, a few days after the red clay Grand Slam, another Russian was to capture a Grand Slam title on Wimbledon's grass. Maria Sharapova was the first Russian to take part in the London tournament. She won her first Grand Slam title while she was making her first Grand Slam final appearance.

Top seed No. 13, Maria did not face many difficulties in the first week. She defeated the Croatian Yulia Beygelzimer and a wild-card (the British Anne Keothavong). Then she took advantage of Daniela Hantuchova's withdrawal. From then on, things were more difficult. She had to fight to get a two-set victory against Amy Frazier (6/3, 7/5), a three-set win against Sugiyama (5/7, 7/5, 6/1), another three-set winning match in semi-finals against top seed No. 5 Lindsay Davenport (2/6, 7/6, 6/1), and eventually reach the final against the top seed No. 1, who is used to this Centre Court. Serena Williams wanted to complete a hat-trick of Wimbledon successes. She had captured the title in the past two years, each time defeating her sister Venus. Serena Williams won a total of six Grand Slam trophies. Let's quote them in a chronological order: the US Open in 1999; Roland-Garros, Wimbledon and the US Open in 2002; and in 2003, the Australian Open followed by Wimbledon. Serena had lost only one Grand Slam final match before this one. It was in 2001 at the US Open against her sister. But Serena is not the same as she was last year. She has been out of the courts for more than eight months due to knee surgery. She did not play one single official match between her July 2003 Wimbledon victory and her bright comeback in March 2004 in Miami. During all that

" I thought that winning Wimbledon was just my dream, and now, of course, my goal is to be No.1 in the world. "

Maria Sharapova

" I was not surprised to see her fight so hard. I watched her; I knew she would not give up. She is a bit like me. "

Serena Williams

Maria Sharapova

time she must have lost some her abilities. At Roland-Garros, she ousted in quarterfinals. Some may say it is great success to have gone this far in Wimbledon but Serena wants more: "I'll sit here and say that, yeah, it is a solid achievement for me because it's been a while. I don't know how many people can come back and do so well. But for me, it is not good enough." Serena is hard on herself. She has been incredible during Wimbledon's two weeks of competition. She found her form at these Championships. She won over Capriati in quarterfinals 6/1, 6/1 and bulldozed her way to the semi-finals against Amelie Mauresmo. Although the Frenchwoman was very close to a second Grand Slam final (after the Australian Open in 1999), she was defeated by Serena who showed everyone she wanted this victory more than anything. Amelie believed in her own victory until the score reached 7/6, 3/1. But then, she was weakened by another physical pain - in her back this time.

Before entering the court on the last day, the pressure seemed to be higher for the young Sharapova than for the star Serena. Nevertheless, Maria was speaking like a real champion: "Which other girl of my age would not want to experience what I am living now? If I feel pressure, I just have to leave, she said. I am 17 years old. What do I have to lose in this world?" Not much indeed. She was in a winning mood. After the match, we all changed our minds; Serena could not resist the pressure: "I was too nervous", she admitted. "I wanted to capture it more than anything."

Born in Siberia, Sharapova trained in the Nick Bollettieri Academy in Florida. Much had been of Sharapova's striking blonde looks, with comparisons drawn between her and countrywoman Anna Kournikova. This comparison remains a physical one because unlike Kournikova, Sharapova wins. She wins matches or even better, she wins tournaments. Just before Wimbledon, she had won in Birmingham, which brought the total amount of

her victories on grass to 12, against no defeat. It is the fourth title in her (short) career together with that of Tokyo, Quebec and Birmingham (three Tier III). At the age of seventeen years and two months, Maria Sharapova became the second youngest player to capture a Grand Slam title since Open Era after Martina Hingis, who had won the title in 1997 at the age of 16 years and nine months old. Thanks to this title she is now in the world top 10. Therefore, from now on, Maria Sharapova will also be looked at for her tennis. "It's amazing, really", she said. "I'm absolutely speechless. I never, never in my life expected this to happen so fast. And it's always been my dream to come here and to win. But it was never in my mind that I would do it this year." Serena Williams nicely concluded: "I was really happy for Maria because I know what you feel at that time. There is nothing better! " Others did not have the chance to experience this feeling. But the attitude is the right one. Let us draw your attention

Tatiana Golovin

4

Amelie Mauresmo played her fourth Grand Slam's semi-final matches. In Wimbledon, she lost only one set on her way to reach it. It was against the Argentine Paola Suarez in quarterfinals.

on the performances of Karolina Sprem, 19-year-old, and of Tatiana Golovin, 16-year-old. The Croatian ousted top seed No. 3 Venus Williams as from the second round and then sailed into quarterfinals defeating Meghann Shaughnessy and Magdalena Maleeva. As for the French, she defeated Francesca Schiavone (top seed No. 18) in the second round (6/1, 6/0). For the second time this season, she made it to a Grand Slam third round, where she was defeated by defending champ Serena Williams on the Centre Court (6/2,

6/1). Roland-Garros's two finalists did not stand out in this Wimbledon tournament. They could not perform as well as they did in Paris. Myskina was defeated in the third round by Amy Frazier and Elena Dementieva in the first round by Sandra Kleinova.
The final score was 6/1, 6/4, but it was not the highlight of the match. Most important was the champ's spirit: "I did not even think it was a final and whom I was playing, Maria said. I was focused on my task and I knew that my strength was with me."

Karolina Sprem

126

Serena Williams set her own record with a serve measuring 126mph during the third round against the French Tatiana Golovin (6/2, 6/1). The official record was held by her sister Venus with a serve of 127mph, set in Zurich in 1999.

Martina Still Enjoys it

Martina Navratilova won only one singles match this year but it is not bad at all. At the age of 47, she made a great impression, just like she did in the good old days on court No. 2. On the other side of the net, the 25-year-old Columbian Catalina Castano, world 102nd-ranked, seemed less quick on her feet that her opponent, who played her first match here 31 years ago. "Some people wonder why I'm doing this, others think it's just great. I guess the answer is, because I still can. It is not a question of age. It is a question of enjoying it. My message is 'If you do not enjoy it, then give up!'" In any case, we sure still enjoy watching her having fun on a tennis court. Even at her age.

WIMBLEDON

"Somehow I feel even more joy this year because I had so much pressure going into this tournament."

Roger Federer

Roger's Supremacy

We can say for sure that rain was the main character of the Wimbledon movie. Minor parts were brilliantly played by world No. 1 and No. 2. At the end, Roger Federer won over Andy Roddick.

"In our job, the ideal is to face the best in the world. A final in Wimbledon against World No. 1 Roger, you can not dream of anything better." But Andy Roddick's dream stopped there. The world No. 1 Roger Federer played once again better tennis than him, world No. 2. In the final match, the American was overwhelmed by the Swiss. However, this final match was much more interesting than that played in the women's competition, where Maria Sharapova won over Serena Williams. Last year's winner, Federer, captured the third Grand Slam title in his career (after Wimbledon in 2003 and the Australian Open in 2004). He is the first player, after Agassi in 1999, to win two Grand Slams in a same season. Three Grand Slam finals, three victories. Federer is capable of winning when he has to. He won the last eight finals he played. The last one dated back to 2003 in Gstaad. Federer did very well. All his opponents had no choice but to surrender. Alex Bogdanovic, Alejandro Falla, Thomas Johansson, Ivo Karlovic, Leyton Hewitt (first one to take a set from the Swiss in quarterfinals), Sebastien Grosjean in semi-finals, and finally Andy Roddick all had a very bad time against Federer. In semi-finals, Roddick defeated the Croatian Mario Ancic (world No. 63), who had himself beaten Tim Henman in the quarterfinals.
Sunday July 4, 2004 Federer played his best enemy, Roddick. Before this seventh meeting between the two men, Federer won five victories against one defeat. However, this final match was not a particularly fun time for the Swiss. He said: "I don't know if the backhand was really my problem, you know. I just thought it was the combination of Andy really playing well and him not allowing me actually to play the way I wanted to. He was hitting off both sides, backhand and forehand, very hard,

" Roger is a great champion and I congratulate him for this victory. I threw the kitchen sink at him but he went to the bathroom and got his tub. "

Andy Roddick

Andy Roddick

Joachim
Johansson

125

The Swede
Joachim Johansson served 125 aces
in only four matches.

and deep into the baseline. All I could do was actually block
the ball back. I couldn't even slice. So that is a credit to
him. He was putting me under pressure."

It is probably rain, which allowed Federer to overcome his
stress. After a second rain delay in the third set, Federer
came out in determined fashion. "Thanks to rain, I started
thinking and I understood I had to be more aggressive in
front of him", he said. But Roddick regrets those rain delays:
"Before the break we were fighting like dogs. I gave all I
had. I was feeling good, I think I was controlling the
situation. Who knows what would have happened without
those breaks?" Without those breaks, maybe Federer would
not have got his backhand back. Maybe the Swiss would
not have been so aggressive. Maybe he would not have
closed the match after 2.30 hours playing. Maybe he would
not have defeated Andy Roddick in four sets 4/6, 7/5, 7/6,
6/4. At the end of the day, Roger captured his sixth title of
the year after the Australian Open, Dubai, Indian Wells,
Hamburg and Halle. Rain did not help the American. Let us
hope that Andy does not wait for stormy weather to show a
stronger resistance to Mister Federer.

Wimbledon's surprise

Florian Mayer, the German Rising Star

"He was world ranked No. 360 in the beginning of the year and now he is in the top 100. He has the ability to enter the top 50." This is the way Michael Stich described the young German Florian Mayer. Even Boris Becker let us know his opinion: "He reminds me Miloslav Mecir. He has an incredible eye-arm coordination. He manages to prejudge and he is able to leave some extraordinary hits." At the age of 21, Florian feels more at ease on red clay. His best performance is the semi-final match in the Estoril tournament. "My favourite surface is red clay, he admits. When arriving here (in Wimbledon), I could not find my marks. I came to have some experience". And Florian did well. He defeated Wayne Arthurs in three sets 7/6, 7/6, 7/6 in the first round. Rather self-confident after defeating Guillermo Coria (4/6, 6/3, 6/3, 6/4), Wayne Ferreira (7/6, 6/3, 6/1), Joachim Johansson (6/7, 7/6, 6/4) he kept on going until quarterfinals. It is the French Sebastien Grosjean who put an end to the crazy race of the German. To reach Grand Slam quarterfinals (especially on grass) is not bad at all for experience.

Goran Ivanisevic   Florian Mayer

4 The first round match between Guillermo Coria and Wesley Moodie was played over four days due to several rain breaks.

0 Before the semi-finals, the American Andy Roddick and the French Sebastien Grosjean had not lost one single set.

Goran Says Good Bye !

The last time Goran Ivanisevic appeared on the Wimbledon grass was to lift the trophy. He had beaten Patrick Rafter in 2001 in five sets at the All England Club after entering as wild-card as he was only world 125th-ranked. Since then, several injuries forced him to stay home. At the age of 32, the Croat made his decision. He will retire, but only after he has defended his Wimbledon title. He won the first round against Mikhail Youzhny and retired once and for all from tennis after having been beaten by Lleyton Hewitt. Goran left competition having won two Olympic medals, 22 titles and a rank of world No. 1.

WIMBLEDON

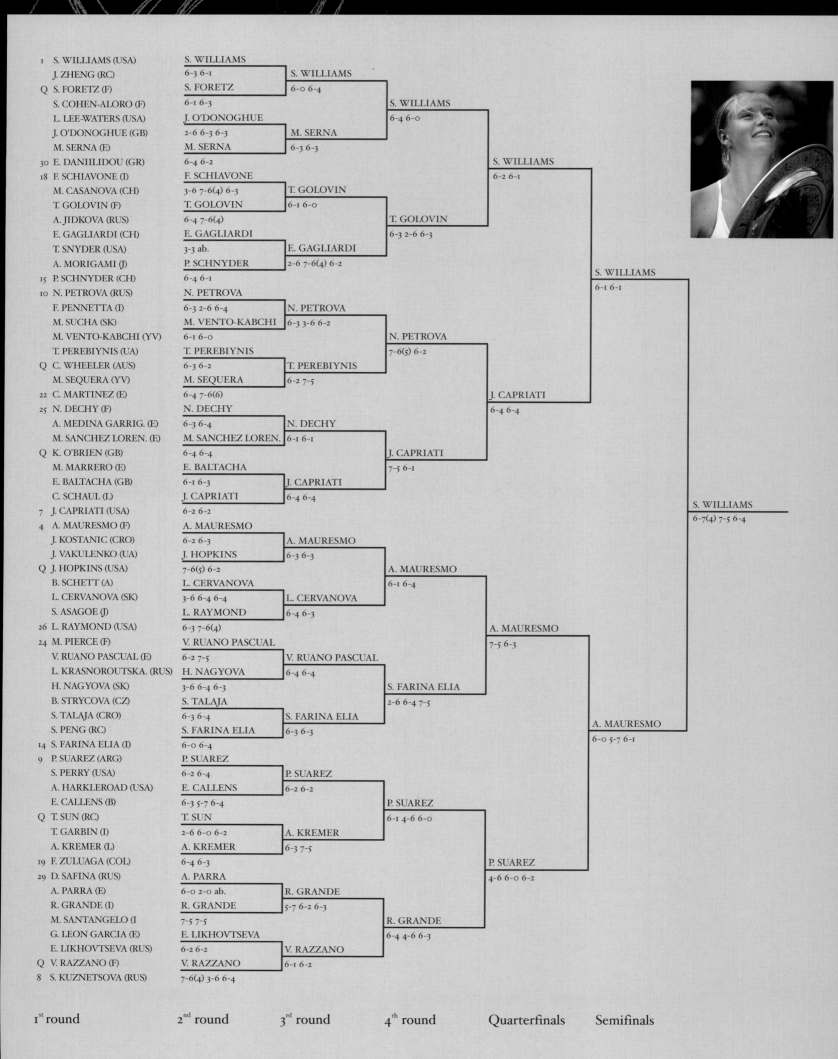

1st round	2nd round	3rd round	4th round	Quarterfinals	Semifinals

1   S. WILLIAMS (USA)
    J. ZHENG (RC)
Q   S. FORETZ (F)
    S. COHEN-ALORO (F)
    L. LEE-WATERS (USA)
    J. O'DONOGHUE (GB)
    M. SERNA (E)
30 E. DANIILIDOU (GR)
18 F. SCHIAVONE (I)
    M. CASANOVA (CH)
    T. GOLOVIN (F)
    A. JIDKOVA (RUS)
    E. GAGLIARDI (CH)
    T. SNYDER (USA)
    A. MORIGAMI (J)
15 P. SCHNYDER (CH)
10 N. PETROVA (RUS)
    F. PENNETTA (I)
    M. SUCHA (SK)
    M. VENTO-KABCHI (YV)
    T. PEREBIYNIS (UA)
Q   C. WHEELER (AUS)
    M. SEQUERA (YV)
22 C. MARTINEZ (E)
25 N. DECHY (F)
    A. MEDINA GARRIG. (E)
    M. SANCHEZ LOREN. (E)
Q   K. O'BRIEN (GB)
    M. MARRERO (E)
    E. BALTACHA (GB)
    C. SCHAUL (L)
7   J. CAPRIATI (USA)
4   A. MAURESMO (F)
    J. KOSTANIC (CRO)
    J. VAKULENKO (UA)
Q   J. HOPKINS (USA)
    B. SCHETT (A)
    L. CERVANOVA (SK)
    S. ASAGOE (J)
26 L. RAYMOND (USA)
24 M. PIERCE (F)
    V. RUANO PASCUAL (E)
    L. KRASNOROUTSKA. (RUS)
    H. NAGYOVA (SK)
    B. STRYCOVA (CZ)
    S. TALAJA (CRO)
    S. PENG (RC)
14 S. FARINA ELIA (I)
9   P. SUAREZ (ARG)
    S. PERRY (USA)
    A. HARKLEROAD (USA)
    E. CALLENS (B)
Q   T. SUN (RC)
    T. GARBIN (I)
    A. KREMER (L)
19 F. ZULUAGA (COL)
29 D. SAFINA (RUS)
    A. PARRA (E)
    R. GRANDE (I)
    M. SANTANGELO (I
    G. LEON GARCIA (E)
    E. LIKHOVTSEVA (RUS)
Q   V. RAZZANO (F)
8   S. KUZNETSOVA (RUS)

2nd round:
S. WILLIAMS 6-3 6-1
S. FORETZ 6-1 6-3
J. O'DONOGHUE 2-6 6-3 6-3
M. SERNA 6-4 6-2
F. SCHIAVONE 3-6 7-6(4) 6-3
T. GOLOVIN 6-4 7-6(4)
E. GAGLIARDI 3-3 ab.
P. SCHNYDER 6-4 6-1
N. PETROVA 6-3 2-6 6-4
M. VENTO-KABCHI 6-1 6-0
T. PEREBIYNIS 6-3 6-2
M. SEQUERA 6-4 7-6(6)
N. DECHY 6-3 6-4
M. SANCHEZ LOREN. 6-4 6-4
E. BALTACHA 6-1 6-3
J. CAPRIATI 6-2 6-2
A. MAURESMO 6-2 6-3
J. HOPKINS 7-6(5) 6-2
L. CERVANOVA 3-6 6-4 6-4
L. RAYMOND 6-3 7-6(4)
V. RUANO PASCUAL 6-2 7-5
H. NAGYOVA 3-6 6-4 6-3
S. TALAJA 6-3 6-4
S. FARINA ELIA 6-0 6-4
P. SUAREZ 6-2 6-4
E. CALLENS 6-3 5-7 6-4
T. SUN 2-6 6-0 6-2
A. KREMER 6-4 6-3
A. PARRA 6-0 2-0 ab.
R. GRANDE 7-5 7-5
E. LIKHOVTSEVA 6-2 6-2
V. RAZZANO 7-6(4) 3-6 6-4

3rd round:
S. WILLIAMS 6-0 6-4
M. SERNA 6-3 6-3
T. GOLOVIN 6-1 6-0
E. GAGLIARDI 2-6 7-6(4) 6-2
N. PETROVA 6-3 3-6 6-2
T. PEREBIYNIS 6-2 7-5
N. DECHY 6-1 6-1
J. CAPRIATI 4-6 6-4
A. MAURESMO 6-3 6-3
L. CERVANOVA 6-4 6-3
V. RUANO PASCUAL 6-4 6-4
S. FARINA ELIA 6-3 6-3
P. SUAREZ 6-2 6-2
A. KREMER 6-3 7-5
R. GRANDE 5-7 6-2 6-3
V. RAZZANO 6-1 6-2

4th round:
S. WILLIAMS 6-4 6-0
T. GOLOVIN 6-3 2-6 6-3
N. PETROVA 7-6(5) 6-2
J. CAPRIATI 7-5 6-1
A. MAURESMO 6-1 6-4
S. FARINA ELIA 2-6 6-4 7-5
P. SUAREZ 6-1 4-6 6-0
R. GRANDE 6-4 4-6 6-3

Quarterfinals:
S. WILLIAMS 6-2 6-1
J. CAPRIATI 6-4 6-4
A. MAURESMO 7-5 6-3
P. SUAREZ 4-6 6-0 6-2

Semifinals:
S. WILLIAMS 6-1 6-1
A. MAURESMO 6-0 5-7 6-1

S. WILLIAMS 6-7(4) 7-5 6-4

Maria SHARAPOVA

6-1 6-4

M. SHARAPOVA
2-6 7-6(5) 6-1

L. DAVENPORT
6-2 6-2

L. DAVENPORT
6-4 6-4

L. DAVENPORT
6-2 6-1

L. DAVENPORT
6-0 1-0 ab.

L. DAVENPORT   L. DAVENPORT (USA) 9
6-2 6-1   D. RANDRIANTEFY (MA)
K. BRANDI   K. BRANDI (PUR)
6-2 6-0   I. BENESOVA (CZ)

T. PANOVA
6-3 6-4

M. WASHINGTON   A. WIDJAJA (IND) Q
6-2 6-1   M. WASHINGTON (USA) Q
T. PANOVA   T. PANOVA (RUS) Q
6-1 6-2   E. LOIT (F) 28

V. ZVONAREVA
6-4 6-2

G. DULKO
3-6 6-3 6-3

G. DULKO   J. DOKIC (YU) 23
6-3 6-3   G. DULKO (RRA)
M. NAVRATILOVA   C. CASTANO (COL)
6-0 6-1   M. NAVRATILOVA (USA)

V. ZVONAREVA
6-1 6-4

S. OBATA   S. OBATA (J)
4-6 6-4 7-5   E. BIRNEROVA (CZ) Q
V. ZVONAREVA   S. STOSUR (AUS)
6-4 6-4   V. ZVONAREVA (RUS) 12

K. SPREM
6-4 6-4

M. MALEEVA
7-5 6-3

D. CHLADKOVA
7-6(5) 6-0

K. SREBOTNIK   A. SMASHNOVA-PIS. (IL) 16
6-4 6-3   K. SREBOTNIK (SLO)
D. CHLADKOVA   M. WEINGARTNER (D)
6-3 6-1   D. CHLADKOVA (CZ)

M. MALEEVA
6-2 6-3

J. CRAYBAS   J. CRAYBAS (USA)
6-4 6-3   C. BLACK (ZW)
M. MALEEVA   V. DOUCHEVINA (RUS)
6-1 7-5   M. MALEEVA (BG) 21

K. SPREM
7-6(5) 7-6(2)

M. SHAUGHNESSY
6-4 4-6 10-8

M. SHAUGHNESSY   M. SHAUGHNESSY (USA) 32
7-6(3) 7-6(0)   M. IRVIN (USA)
N. LLAGOSTERA VI.   P. MANDULA (H)
6-3 6-3   N. LLAGOSTERA VI. (E) Q

K. SPREM
7-6(5) 7-6(6)

K. SPREM   K. SPREM (CRO)
2-6 6-1 6-4   L. GRANVILLE (USA)
V. WILLIAMS   M. MIKAELIAN (CH)
6-3 6-0   V. WILLIAMS (USA) 3

M. SHARAPOVA
5-7 7-5 6-1

A. SUGIYAMA
6-3 7-5

T. TANASUGARN
6-2 6-4

T. TANASUGARN
6-3 6-3

S. KLEINOVA   E. DEMENTIEVA (RUS) 6
6-4 1-6 6-4   S. KLEINOVA (CZ)
T. TANASUGARN   A. GROENEFELD (D)
6-2 6-0   T. TANASUGARN (T)

A. MOLIK
7-5 6-4

T. ASHLEY   T. PISNIK (SLO)
2-6 6-1 7-5   T. ASHLEY (USA)
A. MOLIK   M. CZINK (H)
6-1 6-4   A. MOLIK (AUS) 27

A. SUGIYAMA
6-1 6-2

M. BARTOLI
6-3 6-3

M. BARTOLI   C. RUBIN (USA)
7-6(5) 6-3   M. BARTOLI (F)
M. CAMERIN   M. CAMERIN (I)
7-5 6-2   A. BARNA (D)

A. SUGIYAMA
6-4 6-4

K. KOUKALOVA   J. JANKOVIC (YU)
3-6 6-1 6-4   K. KOUKALOVA (CZ)
A. SUGIYAMA   A. JANES (GB)
3-6 6-2 6-3   A. SUGIYAMA (J) 11

M. SHARAPOVA
6-4 7-5

M. SHARAPOVA
6-3 6-1

M. SHARAPOVA
6-4 6-0

M. SHARAPOVA   M. SHARAPOVA (RUS) 13
6-2 6-1   Y. BEYGELZIMER (UA) Q
A. KEOTHAVONG   A. KEOTHAVONG (GB)
6-3 6-1   N. PRATT (AUS)

D. HANTUCHOVA
w.o*

D. HANTUCHOVA   D. HANTUCHOVA (SK)
6-1 6-4   S. REEVES (USA)
E. BOVINA   E. GALLOVITS (RU) Q
6-1 6-2   E. BOVINA (RUS) 20

A. FRAZIER
4-6 6-4 6-4

A. FRAZIER
6-2 3-6 8-6

A. FRAZIER   A. FRAZIER (USA) 31
6-1 6-4   M. KIRILENKO (RUS)
E. WEBLEY-SMITH   E. WEBLEY-SMITH (GB) Q
7-6(2) 6-4   S. BELTRAME (F)

A. MYSKINA
5-7 6-2 6-4

A. KAPROS   M. JUGIC-SALKIC (BIH) Q
6-4 2-6 6-3   A. KAPROS (H)
A. MYSKINA   L. KURHAJCOVA (SK)
7-5 6-1   A. MYSKINA (RUS) 2

Semifinals	Quarterfinals	4th round	3rd round	2nd round	1st round

*walkover

WIMBLEDON

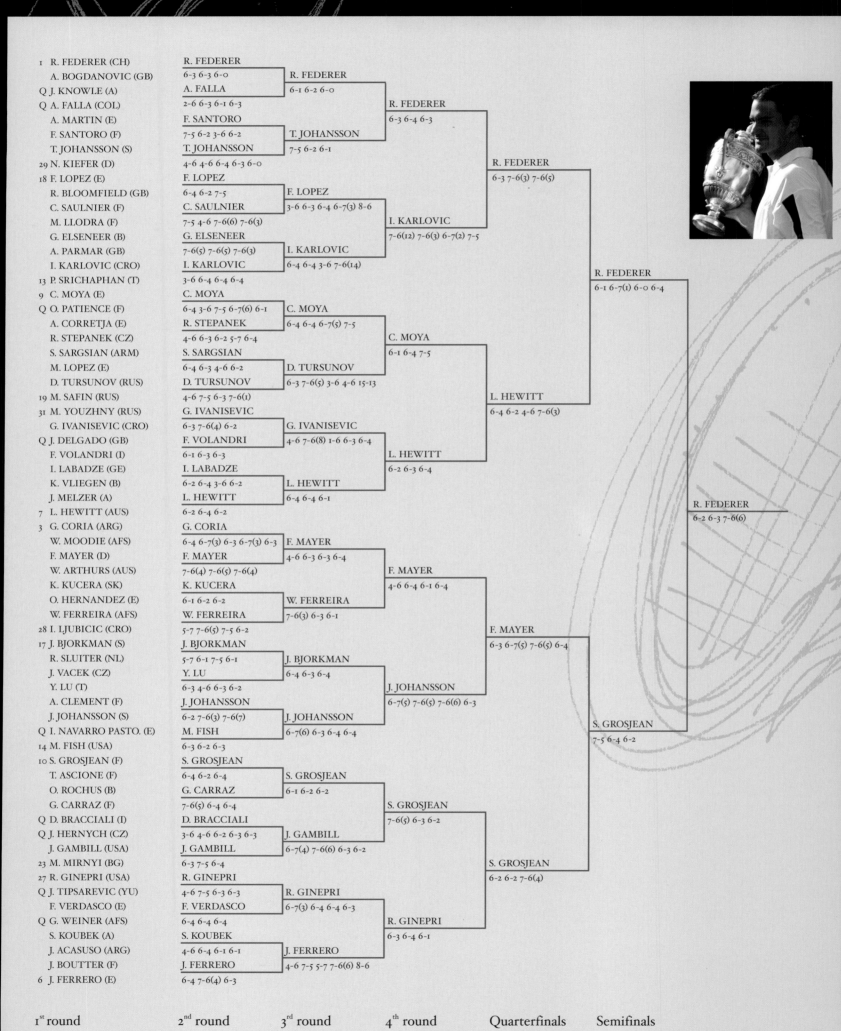

1st round	2nd round	3rd round	4th round	Quarterfinals	Semifinals

1st round

1 R. FEDERER (CH)
A. BOGDANOVIC (GB)
Q J. KNOWLE (A)
Q A. FALLA (COL)
A. MARTIN (E)
F. SANTORO (F)
T. JOHANSSON (S)
29 N. KIEFER (D)
18 F. LOPEZ (E)
R. BLOOMFIELD (GB)
C. SAULNIER (F)
M. LLODRA (F)
G. ELSENEER (B)
A. PARMAR (GB)
I. KARLOVIC (CRO)
13 P. SRICHAPHAN (T)
9 C. MOYA (E)
Q O. PATIENCE (F)
A. CORRETJA (E)
R. STEPANEK (CZ)
S. SARGSIAN (ARM)
M. LOPEZ (E)
D. TURSUNOV (RUS)
19 M. SAFIN (RUS)
31 M. YOUZHNY (RUS)
G. IVANISEVIC (CRO)
Q J. DELGADO (GB)
F. VOLANDRI (I)
I. LABADZE (GE)
K. VLIEGEN (B)
J. MELZER (A)
7 L. HEWITT (AUS)
3 G. CORIA (ARG)
W. MOODIE (AFS)
F. MAYER (D)
W. ARTHURS (AUS)
K. KUCERA (SK)
O. HERNANDEZ (E)
W. FERREIRA (AFS)
28 I. LJUBICIC (CRO)
17 J. BJORKMAN (S)
R. SLUITER (NL)
J. VACEK (CZ)
Y. LU (T)
A. CLEMENT (F)
J. JOHANSSON (S)
Q I. NAVARRO PASTO. (E)
14 M. FISH (USA)
10 S. GROSJEAN (F)
T. ASCIONE (F)
O. ROCHUS (B)
G. CARRAZ (F)
Q D. BRACCIALI (I)
Q J. HERNYCH (CZ)
J. GAMBILL (USA)
23 M. MIRNYI (BG)
27 R. GINEPRI (USA)
Q J. TIPSAREVIC (YU)
F. VERDASCO (E)
Q G. WEINER (AFS)
S. KOUBEK (A)
J. ACASUSO (ARG)
J. BOUTTER (F)
6 J. FERRERO (E)

2nd round

R. FEDERER
6-3 6-3 6-0
A. FALLA
2-6 6-3 6-1 6-3
F. SANTORO
7-5 6-2 3-6 6-2
T. JOHANSSON
4-6 4-6 6-4 6-3 6-0
F. LOPEZ
6-4 6-2 7-5
C. SAULNIER
7-5 4-6 7-6(6) 7-6(3)
G. ELSENEER
7-6(5) 7-6(5) 7-6(3)
I. KARLOVIC
3-6 6-4 6-4 6-4
C. MOYA
6-4 3-6 7-5 6-7(6) 6-1
R. STEPANEK
4-6 6-3 6-2 5-7 6-4
S. SARGSIAN
6-4 6-3 4-6 6-2
D. TURSUNOV
4-6 7-5 6-3 7-6(1)
G. IVANISEVIC
6-3 7-6(4) 6-2
F. VOLANDRI
6-1 6-3 6-3
I. LABADZE
6-2 6-4 3-6 6-2
L. HEWITT
6-2 6-4 6-2
G. CORIA
6-4 6-7(3) 6-3 6-7(3) 6-3
F. MAYER
7-6(4) 7-6(5) 7-6(4)
K. KUCERA
6-1 6-2 6-2
W. FERREIRA
5-7 7-6(5) 7-5 6-2
J. BJORKMAN
5-7 6-1 7-5 6-1
Y. LU
6-3 4-6 6-3 6-2
J. JOHANSSON
6-2 7-6(3) 7-6(7)
M. FISH
6-3 6-2 6-3
S. GROSJEAN
6-4 6-2 6-4
G. CARRAZ
7-6(5) 6-4 6-4
D. BRACCIALI
3-6 4-6 6-2 6-3 6-3
J. GAMBILL
6-3 7-5 6-4
R. GINEPRI
4-6 7-5 6-3 6-3
F. VERDASCO
6-4 6-4 6-4
S. KOUBEK
4-6 6-4 6-1 6-1
J. FERRERO
6-4 7-6(4) 6-3

3rd round

R. FEDERER
6-1 6-2 6-0
T. JOHANSSON
7-5 6-2 6-1
F. LOPEZ
3-6 6-3 6-4 6-7(3) 8-6
I. KARLOVIC
6-4 6-4 3-6 7-6(14)
C. MOYA
6-4 6-4 6-7(5) 7-5
D. TURSUNOV
6-3 7-6(5) 3-6 4-6 15-13
G. IVANISEVIC
4-6 7-6(8) 1-6 6-3 6-4
L. HEWITT
6-4 6-4 6-1
F. MAYER
4-6 6-3 6-3 6-4
W. FERREIRA
7-6(3) 6-3 6-1
J. BJORKMAN
6-4 6-3 6-4
J. JOHANSSON
6-7(6) 6-3 6-4 6-4
S. GROSJEAN
6-1 6-2 6-2
J. GAMBILL
6-7(4) 7-6(6) 6-3 6-2
R. GINEPRI
6-7(3) 6-4 6-4 6-3
J. FERRERO
4-6 7-5 5-7 7-6(6) 8-6

4th round

R. FEDERER
6-3 6-4 6-3
I. KARLOVIC
7-6(12) 7-6(3) 6-7(2) 7-5
C. MOYA
6-1 6-4 7-5
L. HEWITT
6-2 6-3 6-4
F. MAYER
4-6 6-4 6-1 6-4
J. JOHANSSON
6-7(5) 7-6(5) 7-6(6) 6-3
S. GROSJEAN
7-6(5) 6-3 6-2
R. GINEPRI
6-3 6-4 6-1

Quarterfinals

R. FEDERER
6-3 7-6(3) 7-6(5)
L. HEWITT
6-4 6-2 4-6 7-6(3)
F. MAYER
6-3 6-7(5) 7-6(5) 6-4
S. GROSJEAN
6-2 6-2 7-6(4)

Semifinals

R. FEDERER
6-1 6-7(1) 6-0 6-4
S. GROSJEAN
7-5 6-4 6-2

R. FEDERER
6-2 6-3 7-6(6)

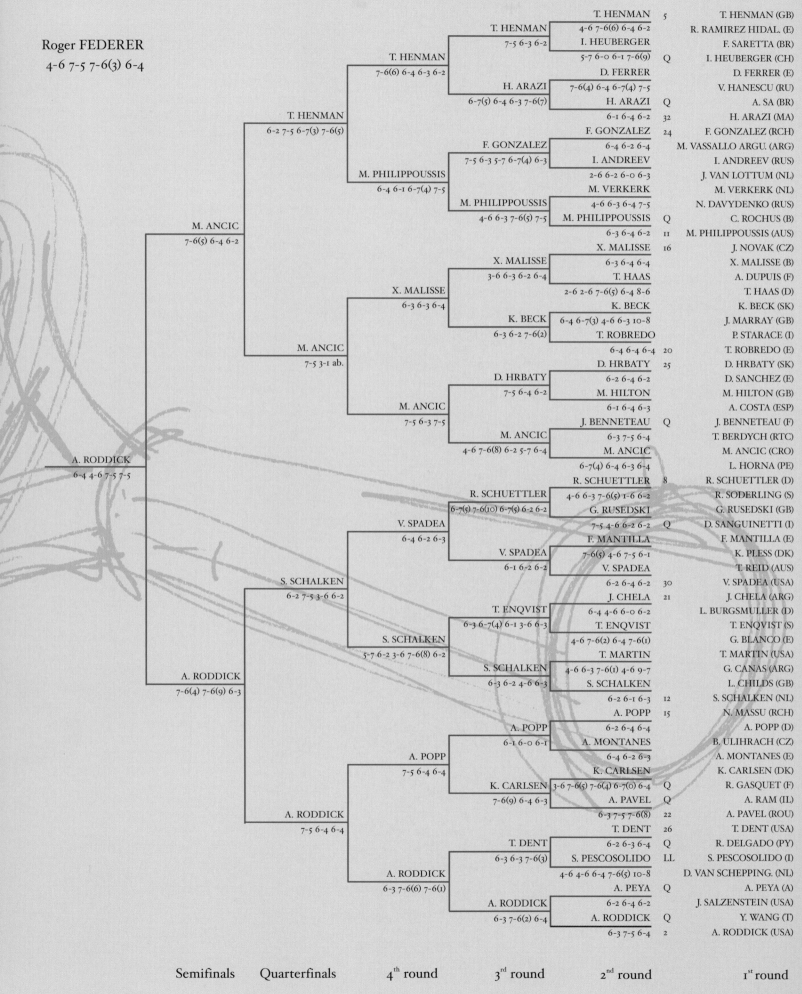

Roger FEDERER
4-6 7-5 7-6(3) 6-4

M. ANCIC
7-6(5) 6-4 6-2

T. HENMAN
6-2 7-5 6-7(3) 7-6(5)

M. ANCIC
7-5 3-1 ab.

A. RODDICK
6-4 4-6 7-5 7-5

S. SCHALKEN
6-2 7-5 3-6 6-2

A. RODDICK
7-6(4) 7-6(9) 6-3

T. HENMAN
7-6(6) 6-4 6-3 6-2

M. PHILIPPOUSSIS
6-4 6-1 6-7(4) 7-5

X. MALISSE
6-3 6-3 6-4

M. ANCIC
7-5 6-3 7-5

V. SPADEA
6-4 6-2 6-3

S. SCHALKEN
5-7 6-2 3-6 7-6(8) 6-2

A. POPP
7-5 6-4 6-4

A. RODDICK
7-5 6-4 6-4

T. HENMAN
7-5 6-3 6-2

H. ARAZI
6-7(5) 6-4 6-3 7-6(7)

F. GONZALEZ
7-5 6-3 5-7 6-7(4) 6-3

M. PHILIPPOUSSIS
4-6 6-3 7-6(5) 7-5

X. MALISSE
3-6 6-3 6-2 6-4

K. BECK
3-6 6-2 7-6(2)

D. HRBATY
7-5 6-4 6-2

M. ANCIC
4-6 7-6(8) 6-2 5-7 6-4

R. SCHUETTLER
6-7(5) 7-6(10) 6-7(5) 6-2 6-2

V. SPADEA
6-1 6-2 6-2

T. ENQVIST
6-3 6-7(4) 6-1 3-6 6-3

S. SCHALKEN
6-3 6-2 4-6 6-3

A. POPP
6-1 6-0 6-1

K. CARLSEN
7-6(9) 6-4 6-3

T. DENT
6-3 6-3 7-6(3)

A. RODDICK
6-3 7-6(6) 7-6(1)

T. HENMAN
4-6 7-6(6) 6-4 6-2

I. HEUBERGER
5-7 6-0 6-1 7-6(9)

D. FERRER
7-6(4) 6-4 6-7(4) 7-5

H. ARAZI
6-1 6-4 6-2

F. GONZALEZ
6-4 6-2 6-4

I. ANDREEV
2-6 6-2 6-0 6-3

M. VERKERK
4-6 6-3 6-4 7-5

M. PHILIPPOUSSIS
6-3 6-4 6-2

X. MALISSE
6-3 6-4 6-4

T. HAAS
2-6 2-6 7-6(5) 6-4 8-6

K. BECK
6-4 6-7(3) 4-6 6-3 10-8

T. ROBREDO
6-4 6-4 6-4

D. HRBATY
6-2 6-4 6-2

M. HILTON
6-1 6-4 6-3

J. BENNETEAU
6-3 7-5 6-4

M. ANCIC
6-7(4) 6-4 6-3 6-4

R. SCHUETTLER
4-6 6-3 7-6(5) 1-6 6-2

G. RUSEDSKI
7-5 4-6 6-2 6-2

F. MANTILLA
7-6(5) 4-6 7-5 6-1

V. SPADEA
6-2 6-4 6-2

J. CHELA
6-4 4-6 6-0 6-2

T. ENQVIST
4-6 7-6(2) 6-4 7-6(1)

T. MARTIN
4-6 6-3 7-6(1) 4-6 9-7

S. SCHALKEN
6-2 6-1 6-3

A. POPP
6-2 6-4 6-4

A. MONTANES
6-4 6-2 6-3

K. CARLSEN
3-6 7-6(5) 7-6(4) 6-7(0) 6-4

A. PAVEL
6-3 7-5 7-6(8)

T. DENT
6-2 6-3 6-4

S. PESCOSOLIDO
4-6 4-6 6-4 7-6(5) 10-8

A. PEYA
6-2 6-4 6-2

A. RODDICK
6-3 7-5 6-4

T. HENMAN	5	T. HENMAN (GB)
		R. RAMIREZ HIDAL. (E)
		F. SARETTA (BR)
I. HEUBERGER	Q	I. HEUBERGER (CH)
D. FERRER		D. FERRER (E)
		V. HANESCU (RU)
H. ARAZI	Q	A. SA (BR)
	32	H. ARAZI (MA)
F. GONZALEZ	24	F. GONZALEZ (RCH)
		M. VASSALLO ARGU. (ARG)
I. ANDREEV		I. ANDREEV (RUS)
		J. VAN LOTTUM (NL)
M. VERKERK		M. VERKERK (NL)
		N. DAVYDENKO (RUS)
M. PHILIPPOUSSIS	Q	C. ROCHUS (B)
	11	M. PHILIPPOUSSIS (AUS)
X. MALISSE	16	J. NOVAK (CZ)
		X. MALISSE (B)
		A. DUPUIS (F)
T. HAAS		T. HAAS (D)
K. BECK		K. BECK (SK)
		J. MARRAY (GB)
T. ROBREDO		P. STARACE (I)
	20	T. ROBREDO (E)
D. HRBATY	25	D. HRBATY (SK)
		D. SANCHEZ (E)
M. HILTON		M. HILTON (GB)
		A. COSTA (ESP)
J. BENNETEAU	Q	J. BENNETEAU (F)
		T. BERDYCH (RTC)
M. ANCIC		M. ANCIC (CRO)
		L. HORNA (PE)
R. SCHUETTLER	8	R. SCHUETTLER (D)
		R. SODERLING (S)
G. RUSEDSKI		G. RUSEDSKI (GB)
	Q	D. SANGUINETTI (I)
F. MANTILLA		F. MANTILLA (E)
		K. PLESS (DK)
V. SPADEA		T. REID (AUS)
	30	V. SPADEA (USA)
J. CHELA	21	J. CHELA (ARG)
		L. BURGSMULLER (D)
T. ENQVIST		T. ENQVIST (S)
		G. BLANCO (E)
T. MARTIN		T. MARTIN (USA)
		G. CANAS (ARG)
S. SCHALKEN		L. CHILDS (GB)
	12	S. SCHALKEN (NL)
A. POPP	15	N. MASSU (RCH)
		A. POPP (D)
A. MONTANES		B. ULIHRACH (CZ)
		A. MONTANES (E)
K. CARLSEN		K. CARLSEN (DK)
	Q	R. GASQUET (F)
A. PAVEL	Q	A. RAM (IL)
	22	A. PAVEL (ROU)
T. DENT	26	T. DENT (USA)
	Q	R. DELGADO (PY)
S. PESCOSOLIDO	LL	S. PESCOSOLIDO (I)
		D. VAN SCHEPPING. (NL)
A. PEYA	Q	A. PEYA (A)
		J. SALZENSTEIN (USA)
A. RODDICK	Q	Y. WANG (T)
	2	A. RODDICK (USA)

The finalists (statistics dated July 5, 2004)

Maria Sharapova

Russia
Birthdate: April 19, 1987
Birthplace: Nyagan, Russia (Siberia)
Height: 6'
Weight: 130 lbs.
Plays: Right-handed
Pro since: 2001
List of awards: 4 titles including 1 Grand Slam (Wimbledon 2004)

Serena Williams

United States of America
Birthdate: September 26, 1981
Birthplace: Saginaw, Michigan, USA
Height: 5'9"
Weight: 130 lbs.
Plays: Right-handed
Pro since: 1995
List of Awards: 25 titles, including 6 Grand Slams (Australian Open 2003, Roland-Garros 2002, Wimbledon 2002 and 2003, US Open 1999 and 2002)

Roger Federer

Switzerland
Birthdate: August 8, 1981
Birthplace: Basel, Switzerland
Height: 6'1"
Weight: 177 lbs.
Plays: Right-handed
Pro since: 1998
Best ranking: No. 1 (February 2, 2004)
List of awards: 12 titles, including 2 Grand Slams (Wimbledon 2003 and Australian Open 2004)

Andy Roddick

United States
Birthdate: August 30, 1982
Birthplace: Omaha, Nebraska (USA)
Height: 6'2"
Weight: 197 lbs.
Plays: Right-handed
Pro since: 2000
Best ATP ranking: No. 1 (November 3, 2003)
List of Awards: 14 titles, including 1 Grand Slam (US Open 2003)

Cara and Wayne Black

The Girls

Katerina is Older than Maria

Katerina Bondarenko is from Ukraine. She was born on August 8, 1986 in Krejery Rig, Ukraine. She is 5'9 1/4" and weighs 132 lbs. She captured her first grass Grand Slam title by beating the Yugoslavian Ana Ivanovic in final 6/4, 6/7, 6/2. In semifinals, she defeated the top favourite Michaela Krajicek (half-sister of Richard, champion in Wimbledon in 1996), which is has to be considered as a nice performance even if she is older than women's champ, Maria Sharapova.

The Boys

Monfils is World Champion

The Australian Open, Roland-Garros and Wimbledon, all of them in one single season. The French Gaël Monfils made certain to become the Junior world No. 1 at the end of 2004. Even if he said he does not like grass courts too much, he dominated everyone during the whole tournament, losing only one set in the second round against Marocco's Mehdi Ziani. In the final, he defeated the British Miles Kasiri 7/5, 7/6. He is now able to equal Stefan Edberg's record, who had won the Grand Slam in 1983. To do so, he has to go on and capture the equivalent event at Flushing Meadows. But from his point of view, it is not a goal. He is already focussed on his future, when he will be playing with the "Men". It should be soon enough: he will be playing his first men's tournament in the 'Open de Moselle' next October.

Women's Doubles

Without Clijsters, Sugiyama Lost her Title

Cara Black (Zimbabwe) and Rennae Stubbs (Australia) had already been successful this year in Sydney and Tokyo, but Wimbledon was their first Grand Slam title together. Black celebrated her first Grand Slam victory in women's doubles while Stubbs captured her second title on the London grass, which is also her fourth Grand Slam doubles title. Together they defeated the South-African Liezel Huber (first final) and the Japanese Ai Sugiyama (who was there to defend the title she captured last year with the Belgian Kim Clijsters) in two sets 6/3, 7/6.

Mixed Doubles

Two Crowns for Cara Black

Cara Black just won her first Grand Slam title in the women's doubles. Moreover she ended the two London weeks with a second title in mixed doubles. Together with her brother Wayne, the Zimbabwean pair became the third duo brother-sister to win Wimbledon mixed doubles title. John and Tracy Austin (en 1980) and Cyril Suk/Helena Sukova (in 1996 and 1997) had captured it before them. Cara and Wayne saved six match points in the second set tiebreak to eventually defeat the Australian Todd Woodbridge and Alicia Molik in three sets. Woodbridge will find compensation in winning the men's doubles.

Men's Doubles

Ninth Title for Todd Woodbridge

Todd Woodbridge, 33-year-old, took part in two finals during this Wimbledon tournament: mixed doubles and men's doubles. In the mixed doubles, he and Alicia Molik failed against the Black family (Cara and Wayne). Woodbridge really wanted to win one of those finals and he did. He paired up with Jonas Björkman (32 years old) and won his third Wimbledon title in a row. Individually, he captured a total of nine (the other titles were captured with Mark Woodforde). It is a record. He is the player who won the highest number of doubles titles in Wimbledon. In the final, Todd and Jonas won over Julian Knowle and Nenad Zimonjic (6/1, 6/4, 4/6, 6/4).

* forfait

Women's Doubles Results

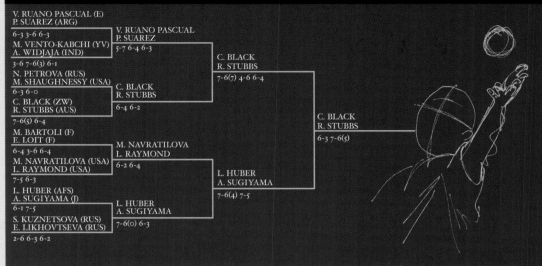

Mixed Doubles Results

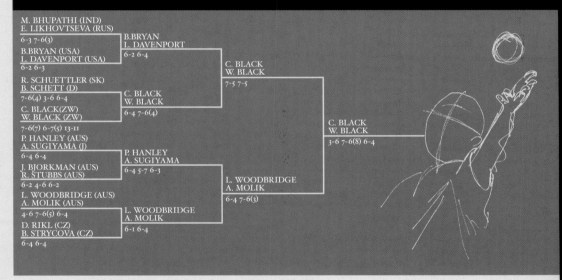

Men's Doubles Results

US and Belgium's Fates Are Sealed

While the French defending champs qualified in Italy for the finals– not without any trouble –, Belgium (last year semi-finalist) and the USA were sent out of the competition before all the final events. Only Russia, Spain, Austria and France managed to sail into semis.

France 3 - Italy 2

Place: Rimini (Italy)
Surface: clay court
Mauresmo's France Ready to Defend Title
The victory was not sealed in advance. The location and the surface were not exactly in the defending champs' favour. In front of clay court specialists, the French players nevertheless managed to win in the heat of Rimini. And this victory was to be thanked once again to a solid performance of the French star player, Amelie Mauresmo. She started with a 6/2, 6/1 dominating win over Silvia Farina Elia. Then, Mary Pierce did the same, beating Francesca Schiavone 6/3, 6/4. Therefore, Amelie just had to win the last point to assure qualification. Mauresmo defeated Schiavone 7/6, 6/2. Mission fulfilled. The remaining matches did not matter anymore. Let's even forget about the defeats of Emilie Loit by Farina Elia and of the Pierce-Golovin pair. The latter was playing her first Fed Cup match.

Austria 4 - USA 1

Place: Innsbruck (Austria)
Surface: clay court
Barbara Schwartz: "the Warrior"
The United States were deprived of the Williams sisters and Lindsay Davenport, who were replaced by Chanda Rubin and Lisa Raymond. Good start for Zina Garrison's girls. Rubin took the first point against Barbara Schwartz (6/1, 5/7, 6/4). Then, Austria evened with the victory of Barbara Schett over Raymond. It was Schett's 29th Fed Cup victory. The day after, Schett was back, facing Rubin. The last point was taken by Schett, who had lost the first day in a three-set match. Schwartz met some difficulties against Lisa Raymond 7/6, 4/6, 10/8. In total, Barbara Schwartz, who had hardly played any competitive tennis over the past eighteen months, has spent nearly six hours on the court in the past two days.

Russia 4 - Argentine 1

Place: Buenos Aires (Argentine)
Surface: clay court
Myskina Relieved Her Team
Russia is growing up. With three singles players ranked in the world top 15, 2003 semi-finalists arrived in Buenos Aires very confident. Although Russia lost the first point of the meeting (defeat of Svetlana Kuznetsova by Gisela Dunko), Roland-Garros winner Anastasia Myskina won the next two points allowing her country to sail into semis (victory over Natalia Gussoni 6/3, 6/0 and Gisela Dulko 6/1, 7/5). Vera Zvonareva took care of the qualifying point by winning over Mariana Diaz-Oliva. The pair Kuznetsova/Likhovtseva was crowning the day, clinching a win over Dulko/Tarabini (6/2, 5/7, 6/4).

Opposite: Anabel Medina and Virginia Ruano Pascual.

Spain 3 - Belgium 2

Place: Jerez de la Frontera (Spain)
Surface: clay court
Belgium Believed In Qualification!
Playing without Justine Henin-Hardenne and Kim Clijsters, the Belgian team did utmost to get it. Kirsten Flipkens and Els Callens staked the Belgians to the early led. The first defeated Anabel Medina Garrigues (7/6, 1/6, 6/2) and the latter won over Virginia Ruano Pascual (2/6, 6/4, 11/9). The Sunday was to be hard for Spain. But Medina Garrigues and Maria Sanchez Lorenzo reacted in front of Callens (6/4, 6/0) and Flipkens (6/3, 6/4). The doubles match put an end to Belgium's hopes and a start to Spain's confidence. Medina Garrigues and Ruano Pascual played the Flipkens/Callens duo and sent their country to the final step (6/3, 6/2).

Anastasia Myskina

Amélie Mauresmo

Roger Upset Andy

The Swiss Roger Federer won for the seventh time in eight matches against the American Andy Roddick. The world No.1 won his eighth title this year by defeating Andy Roddick at the Canadian Open.

Let us start with some explanation on this Open. This year, the Canadian Open took place in Toronto (every other year, the tournament takes place in Montreal, interchanging with the WTA Race). This Open is a Masters Series, that is, one of the nine most important tournaments after the four Grand Slams. This means that such a tournament can make the players win a considerable amount of ATP points and great prizes. But, not long ago, the American Federation created the "US Open Series". The idea of it is to grant a financial bonus to the best three players who piled up the most points over ten pre-US Open tournaments. This occurs both for men

Roger Federer

23 With this victory in Toronto, the Swiss Roger Federer won a total of 23 victories in a row, which means he captured four consecutive titles, including Halle, Wimbledon and Gstaad. He is the first player who achieved this on three different grounds since Björn Borg in 1979.

and women. The money granted is proportional to their results at Flushing Meadows. Two of the three best players this year turned out to be Andy Roddick and Roger Federer, the two finalists of this Canadian Open.

Let us now come to the facts. Sunday, August 1, 2004. The war began: a real service battle. Federer is a sound world No.1 and proved that he could find a way out of any tricky situation. In the first set, 4 games all, he was led 0-40 but he gave the right answer: three aces in a row. That was hard to manage for his opponent. This real barbarian wrestle lasted 1.24 hour and ended with the victory of the Swiss. Once the last shot had been fired, the warriors were tired: "I am exhausted! Really very tired!" Federer said. Andy Roddick, for his part, even had to call the physiotherapist during the first set because his back hurt. Roger

Federer beat the title holder Andy Roddick 7/5, 6/3 on the Swiss national day. He only lost one set that week against the young and promising Thomas Johansson in the semi-finals (4/6, 6/3, 6/2).

Eight! It is Federer's eighth title since the beginning of the year, his fourth successive title, after Halle, Wimbledon and Gstaad. When will he stop winning? He is the first player to win three successive tournaments on three different grounds since Björn Borg in 1979. It is also the seventh victory against the American player out of eight matches. The world No.1 won his revenge for his defeat at Wimbledon, which obviously upset Mister No.2: "Congratulations, Roger but you are starting to become very annoying." And Federer replied the following: "Sorry Andy but I think, in the future, you and I will play many, many more matches, believe me!"

Andy Roddick

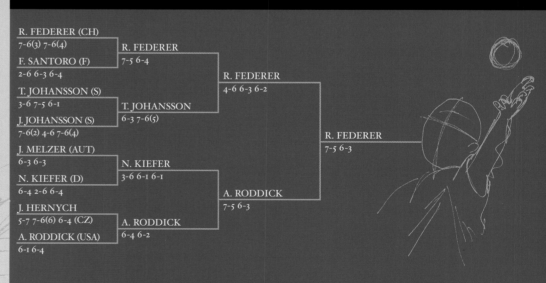

Men's Results

R. FEDERER (CH) 7-6(3) 7-6(4)	R. FEDERER 7-5 6-4	R. FEDERER 4-6 6-3 6-2	R. FEDERER 7-5 6-3
F. SANTORO (F) 2-6 6-3 6-4			
T. JOHANSSON (S) 3-6 7-5 6-1	T. JOHANSSON 6-3 7-6(5)		
J. JOHANSSON (S) 7-6(2) 4-6 7-6(4)			
J. MELZER (AUT) 6-3 6-3	N. KIEFER 3-6 6-1 6-1	A. RODDICK 7-5 6-3	
N. KIEFER (D) 6-4 2-6 6-4			
J. HERNYCH 5-7 7-6(6) 6-4 (CZ)	A. RODDICK 6-4 6-2		
A. RODDICK (USA) 6-1 6-4			

The Californian Grand Slam

After her victories in Stanford and L.A., Lindsay Davenport easily defeated Anastasia Myskina to capture the 43rd title in her career in San Diego, which is also the fifth title she won this year.

The match of the week was not to be the final. As a matter of fact, Lindsay Davenport had to play Anastasia Myskina who was exhausted after the semi-finals she played against countrywoman Vera Zvonareva -the true match of the week. The match lasted two hours and twenty minutes and ended with the final score of 6/2, 6/7 (4), 7/6 (15) - the longest third-set tiebreak in WTA history. Although Zvonareva was just about to defeat Myskina and to reach the top 10, the situation was reversed and it is the Roland-Garros champ who eventually won the match. Therefore, it is easy to understand Zvonareva's physical and mental condition when she stepped on the court to play Davenport in the final. The latter had no

trouble winning against the Russian: 6/1, 6/1. Considering this score, it seems useless to comment this non-match. It was the second tournament in a row, in which the American Lindsay Davenport did not drop a single set, nor in L.A., nor in San Diego. "I feel great. I didn't know what to expect and I've surprised myself. It's been two tournaments without losing a set and I feel in very good shape", she said at the end of the week. This final was the fourteenth consecutive match the American

On the left: Lindsay Davenport

Elena Dementieva   Anastasia Myskina

player won. After Stanford and Los Angeles, Davenport captured the Californian Grand Slam, a record she already achieved in 1998, the year she won the US Open. Thanks to this victory in San Diego, Lindsay Davenport came back to the second place in the world ranking. This made the Russian somehow jealous since she could have reached this ranking for the first time in her career, had she won of course!

What happened to the other players? Serena Williams, who was still suffering from her knee, had to withdraw before the quarterfinal match against Zvonareva. That was a pity for the former No.1 who had reached the final in L.A. the week before. The 2nd seed Amelie Mauresmo lost as from the first round against the Australian Alicia Molik (7/5, 3/6, 6/3). The tennis player who had the most to lose that week did not even take part in the tournament. Last year's finalist, Kim Clijster, slipped from the second to the fifth ranking without playing, due to a wrist injury. Indeed, Davenport replaced her while Mauresmo reached rank No. 3, and Myskina rank No. 4.

66
Lindsay played unbelievably. I would have had to play 200 % to beat her today. 99

Anastasia Myskina

32

It's a record. Never in WTA history had a player won a third set tiebreak in 32 points. Anastasia Myskina did it against countrywomen Vera Zvonareva in the semi-finals in San Diego with a final score of 6/2, 6/7 (4-7), 7/6 (17-15).

* walkover

Women's Results

S. WILLIAMS (USA) 6-4 6-2	V. ZVONAREVA w.o*		
V. ZVONAREVA (RUS) 6-2 6-3		A. MYSKINA 6-2 6-7(4) 7-6(15)	
A. MYSKINA (RUS) 6-1 6-2	A. MYSKINA 7-5 6-2		
M. SHARAPOVA (RUS) 6-0 6-1			L. DAVENPORT 6-1 6-1
A. SUGIYAMA (J) 6-3 6-2	L. DAVENPORT 6-1 6-3		
L. DAVENPORT (USA) 6-1 6-2		L. DAVENPORT 6-2 6-4	
E. DEMENTIEVA (RUS) 6-2 7-6(2)	E. DEMENTIEVA 6-2 6-1		
A. FRAZIER (USA) 3-6 6-3 6-4			

Agassi Is Insatiable

At 34, former world No.1, Andre Agassi, captured
his fifty-ninth title in Cincinnati, his seventeenth
ATP Masters Series field.

Who talked about retiring? 34-year-old Andre Agassi does not
seem to intend to slow down. It is just the opposite, even if
his last appearance in a final dates back to the match where
he was upset by Roger Federer in the Tennis Masters Cup in
Houston last November, the former world No. 1 (top seed No.
11) proved during this week in Cincinnati that even if his
physical condition is not as good as it once was, his mental
strength remains the same. Experience always helps. Holder

On the left:
Lleyton Hewitt

of 58 titles, including 8 Grand Slams, he jumped over Andy Roddick in semi-finals (7/5, 6/7, 7/6) and finally defeated Lleyton Hewitt in final 6/3, 3/6, 6/2. He started winning again after his victory on the U.S. Clay Courts of Houston in April 2003 (against Andy Roddick). He earned US$ 400,000 for the win, giving him 1,283,030 for his career in Cincinnati, with those of 1995 and 1996. As from now on Cincinnati represents a high value for him.

Streak is over. In Cincinnati, Roger Federer puts an end to his series of four titles in a row since he has been eliminated in the third round at Roland-Garros. He was the victim of a Slovakian, whose name is Dominik Hrbaty. As from the first round, he defeated the Swiss, apparently exhausted due to recent feats (1/6, 7/6, 6/4). "Yesterday, when arriving in Cincinnati, I could hardly walk," confirmed the world No.1.

On the French side, Mister Fabrice Santoro fought his second quarterfinals in a row after Toronto the week before. He was defeated by Tommy Robredo (6/2, 6/3) after winning over Robby Ginepri, Mikhail Youzhny and Jonas Björkman.

> " To be honest, I would have preferred to finish this week tired due to playing till the end. "
>
> *Roger Federer*

59 With 59 titles, Andre Agassi is the leading title holder among active players. Far behind, Lleyton Hewitt is second with 21 titles.

Men's Results

F. SANTORO (F) 6-0 6-3				
	T. ROBREDO 6-2 6-3			
T. ROBREDO (E) 7-6(4) 7-6(2)				
		L. HEWITT 6-3 6-2		
M. SAFIN (RUS) 7-6(4) 6-7(3) 6-4				
	L. HEWITT 6-4 6-4			
L. HEWITT (AUS) 6-1 6-4				
			A. AGASSI 6-3 3-6 6-2	
A. AGASSI (USA) 6-3 6-3				
	A. AGASSI 7-6(12) 6-3			
C. MOYA (E) 7-6(5) 4-6 7-6(5)				
		A. AGASSI 7-5 6-7(2) 7-6(2)		
T. HAAS (D) 6-3 5-7 6-4				
	A. RODDICK 6-3 6-3			
A. RODDICK (USA) 6-2 6-3				

Mighty Mauresmo

In the city of Montreal, Amelie Mauresmo celebrated her rise to world No. 2 and her thirteenth career title. There had never been a Frenchwoman with this ranking.

Matches are played one after the other but are not similar. Not at all! The week was kind of a disaster for Amelie Mauresmo, who closed all the matches before final in three sets. Three sets against Tamarine Tanasugarn (6/4, 1/6, 6/2), three against top seed No. 14 Elena Bovina (6/2, 3/6, 6/2) and three against top seed No. 12 Karolina Sprem (3/6, 6/2, 6/4). Only Vera Zvonareva was defeated in two sets (7/6, 6/2). But in the final, the Frenchwoman captured her title with a crushing 6/1, 6/0 win over Likhovtseva. It took her only 51 minutes. We must bear in mind that the Russian was less rested than Amelie Mauresmo since she played her fellow Anastasia Myskina in a tough semi-final match in three sets (6/3, 5/7, 6/4). She also felt fatigue because of the 2.18 hours

marathon match she played against Nadia Petrova in the second round. Then she defeated Francesca Schiavone and Jennifer Capriati in quarterfinals. "It has been a great week for me. I just lacked energy today", she admitted after the last match. It is sad for her as it was her first appearance in the finals of a Tier I tournament. Three Russians in the last four: Anastasia Myskina, Vera Zvonareva and Elena Likhovtseva. Russia currently holds two Grand Slams titles (Myskina in Roland-Garros and Sharapova in Wimbledon), as well as about ten players in the first 50 world ranks. This is the huge surprise this year.

The other surprise is for Amelie Mauresmo, who jumped into the No. 2 spot in the world. It is the first time a French player (men and women) reaches that rank. After Berlin and Rome, the French No. 1 chose Montreal to clinch her third title of the season (third Tier I), the thirteenth of her career.

> " It's a great achievement to be world No. 2 but I want to get to that final spot, that N° 1 rank. That's my goal for two-and-a-half-years now. "
>
> *Amélie Mauresmo*

Elena Likhovtseva

2 With 3 titles in 2004 (Berlin, Rome and Montreal), Amelie Mauresmo became world No. 2. No French player (men and women) had been ranked that high before her.

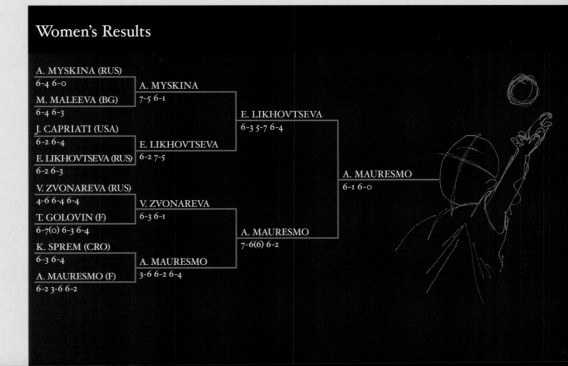

Women's Results

Round 1	Round 2	Quarterfinal	Semifinal	Final
A. MYSKINA (RUS) 6-4 6-0	A. MYSKINA 7-5 6-1			
M. MALEEVA (BG) 6-4 6-3		E. LIKHOVTSEVA 6-3 5-7 6-4		
J. CAPRIATI (USA) 6-2 6-4	E. LIKHOVTSEVA 6-2 7-5			
E. LIKHOVTSEVA (RUS) 6-2 6-3			A. MAURESMO 6-1 6-0	
V. ZVONAREVA (RUS) 4-6 6-4 6-4	V. ZVONAREVA 6-3 6-1			
T. GOLOVIN (F) 6-7(0) 6-3 6-4		A. MAURESMO 7-6(6) 6-2		
K. SPREM (CRO) 6-3 6-4	A. MAURESMO 3-6 6-2 6-4			
A. MAURESMO (F) 6-2 3-6 6-2				

The Human Machine

Ups and downs. The Belgian Justine Henin-Hardenne had an exciting 2004 season. She won great victories, including the Australian Open, Indian Wells and the Olympic Games in Athens, but she also had to face great disappointments like, for example the loss of her World No. 1 rank after the US Open. This is due to a nasty virus that caused a lot of damages.

"I felt like I was a machine", was Justine Henin's statement after winning her Olympic Gold medal. Unfortunately, machines can be infected by viruses, just like human beings. In 2004, Justine Henin-Hardenne experienced it, although the computer was set on 'victory' at the beginning of the year. Indeed, she won her first tournament in Sydney, in January. She beat Amelie Mauresmo in the final with a two-set victory. Of course, she was considered as the top favourite at the

Australian Open since she was No.1. She confirmed her rank in Melbourne where she captured her third Grand Slam title in less than a year. And as usual, she played her compatriot Kim Clijsters in the final, which was their first, but also their last fight on a court for the year. It was there, she lost the only set of the tournament.

When was she going to stop? Not in Dubai, where she won her third title of the year out of three tournaments. That was her seventeenth victory in a row. Yes, Justine had become a real machine: a winning machine.

The machine broke down for the first time in the Doha semi-finals where she was defeated by Svetlana Kuznetsova on March 5, 2004: her first defeat of the year. Even machines have the right to take a break, after all. The purpose of it is to get a better start afterwards.

As soon as the next tournament took place, she got back on track and cruised a while on the road of success. She won Indian Wells, where she had never been lucky. She did not lose one single set and none of her matches lasted more than one hour. Svetlana Kuznetsova (US Open winner to be), Anastasia Myskina (Roland-Garros winner to be) and Lindsay Davenport (who has won five titles this year) had no other choice but admitting that Justine was on another tennis planet.

> " I felt like I was a machine. "
>
> *Justine Henin-Hardenne*

But the Belgian girl was to come back to Earth: she was defeated in the semi-finals by Amelie Mauresmo, on Amelia Island red clay, her favourite ground. A few days later, she announced that she needed some rest. She felt unusually tired and was having trouble recovering from her efforts.

A diagnosis was established after several medical analyses were carried out: she was infected by a cytomegalovirus. This virus that stopped the machine. It is similar to mononucleosis, it has the same symptoms: persisting fatigue and hard recovery. Justine Henin-Hardenne had to skip her preparation period for Roland-Garros. However, she showed up at Porte d'Auteuil in Paris, one month and a half after her last match in Amelia Island. She was ready to defend

SEASON'S OVERVIEW

" I have to gradually rebuild myself.
I will have to make some sacrifices.
This is a new challenge. "

Justine Henin-Hardenne

her first Grand Slam title in the tournament she cherishes. Yes, the machine does have a big heart: Justine wanted to play her tournament at any price. She said to be top fit but couldn't find her marks. She lost the second round match. The Italian Tatiana Garbin sent Justine back to her questions. And to her answers: no, Justine was not that top fit. Again, analyses confirmed it: the World No.1 needed some more rest. The virus was preventing the machine from working at its best.

This time, Justine took the time she needed, with her husband Pierre-Yves Hardenne and her beloved coach Carlos Rodriguez. So, she gave up on Wimbledon, which she had said to be one of her goals for the year 2004.

The other one was Athens, the Olympic Games. Was Justine going to be ready? "I won't make the same mistake as in Roland-Garros" she claimed. She would play only if she had recovered completely. A few weeks before the event was to take place, the news from Wepion, the city where she lives in Belgium, were reassuring: she had resumed training. Pat Etcheberry, her physical coach was taking care of her. The first hums of the engine were heard: the machine attended the Olympic Games, about three months after her disappointment in Paris!

The first rounds reassured the whole of Belgium: Justine Henin-Hardenne managed to find back her game and marks. She confirmed it again in the unexpected semi-finals against Anastasia Myskina. After having given away a 5-1 lead to the Russian in the third set, Justine reversed the situation, as she did in the semi-finals at Roland-Garros and at the US Open in 2003. The talented Justine always gives everything she's got to win a Grand Slam title. Justine eventually captured Gold after playing Amelie Mauresmo in the final.

Justine HENIN-HARDENNE
(Statistics from October 2004)

Birthdate: June 1, 1982
Birthplace: Marloie, Belgium
Height: 5'5 3/4"
Weight: 126 lbs.
Pro since: 1999
Best ranking: 1 (October 20, 2003)
List of awards: 19 singles titles

2004	Sydney, Australian Open, Dubai, Indian Wells, Olympiques Games
2003	Dubai, Charleston, Berlin, Roland-Garros, San Diego, Canadian Open, US Open, Zurich
2002	Berlin, Linz
2001	Gold Coast, Canberra, 's-Hertogenbosch
1999	Anvers

"I felt like I was a machine." Play and win was her leitmotiv at the beginning of the year. Both the virus that was affecting her and Athens, where she lived with other athletes, made her realise about other aspects of life. Tennis was not the only thing that mattered. The machine definitely became human.

Once again, this nasty virus, which effects may be felt for more than a year, came back and spoiled the end of her year. Defeated in the fourth round by Nadia Petrova at Flushing Meadows, she lost her World No. 1 ranking. This will be her last tournament of the season. But from now on, she is able to set her priority straight, as she said: "I wouldn't hesitate a minute to sign for two Grand Slam titles every year." It is true that we have seen ill people feel worse than her. It is also true that, in two years, she captured lots of titles: she is only missing Wimbledon to complete her incredible list of awards.

It may be for 2005. However, in order to reach it, she will have to find the right anti-virus as well as a good anti-Russian. The Eastern girls and Amelie Mauresmo did indeed take advantage from the Belgian absence (Kim being still suffering from her left fist) to take their rank. They already all booked the dates of next year's meetings in their agenda.

> " I would have liked to hear the French national anthem 'the Marseillaise', but the French flag has been well-honoured in this stadium and it is already very well. "
>
> *Amélie Mauresmo,*
> *silver medal*

Justine, the Golden Goddess

A world No. 1 against a world No. 2. What to ask more for such an Olympic final? After two months out of the courts, Justine Henin-Hardenne is back. To take the gold medal Amelie Mauresmo wanted so much.

Absent people are always wrong, especially when it comes to gold. Olympic gold. Kim Clijsters, Serena Williams, Jennifer Capriati, Lindsay Davenport did not move to Athens. The recent Wimbledon champion Maria Sharapova neither. Those girls did not want to climb on the triumphal platform. Other ones will take care of it. In any case only two players may take part in the final, which is perfect as the first two WTA ranked players are on the spot. Gold makes them dream and will make them shine. Justine Henin-Hardenne, Belgium, world No. 1. Amelie Mauresmo, France, world No. 2. They will go through final.

But it was not such a piece of cake. Especially for the Belgian. Sidelined by a viral infection, she had not played a competition match for the past two months. It was in Roland-Garros. It is not a good memory. She wanted to defend her title absolutely. But she was upset in the second round. It was too early. Too early to leave the tournament. Too early to come back into competition. And again when she arrives in Athens, she does not have all her marks. But the first matches will erase any doubt. Justine Henin's opponents will learn to get used again to the world No. 1. In the first round, Barbara Strycova manages to get out of the match with a not so bad 6/3, 6/4. The days go on and Justine spends less and less time on the court. 6/2, 6/1 against Venezuela's Vento-Kabchi. 6/1, 6/0 against Australia's

Akiko Morigami

Amélie Mauresmo and
Justine Henin-Hardenne

Nicole Pratt in the third round. Then Justine
Henin is seen again as the favourite of this
Olympic event.

Her first real test will be the quarterfinals. She
plays Mary Pierce. Mary Pierce, who found her
top level back. Indeed to get there, the
Frenchwoman defeated the young Russian
seed No. 9 Nadia Petrova, but also Venus
Williams, in two sets (6/4, 6/4). But to defeat
Henin, she will be even stronger. The meeting is
beautiful, the match of high standard. Pierce
resists, even if she is forced to give a break in
each set. Justine was stronger. The Belgian
wins 6/4, 6/4.

Without dropping one set along the way, the
Belgian moved into semi-finals. On the other
side of the net, Anastasia Myskina, top seed
No. 3. 2.44 hours later on Justine Henin-
Hardenne is sure to capture a medal. 2.44
hours full of suspense and bounces. As from
the very beginning the match is really tough.
Anastasia Myskina has to run all over the court
but thanks to her excellent footwork, she keeps
on following the level. The world No. 1 level. 7/5
for the Belgian in the first set. 7/5 for the
Russian in the second one. But the last set was
to be even more incredible. The Russian starts
the third set in a top shape. She is quickly
leading 5/1. In front of her, Justine is doubting.
Everybody is jumping into early conclusions.
Justine was not completely top-fit, one thinks.
But everybody was wrong. 5/2, 5/3, 5/4, and
5/5! The Russian served two match points. The
Russian missed the opportunity. Some minutes
later, her opponent serves. Justine leads 7/6
and has a first match point. This last point was
impressive, representative of the whole duel.
Thirty-five racket shots were performed totally
freely, as if both players were not aware of the
bet. The last hit is for the Belgian: a winner
backhand along the line. That's over; the
Belgian goes to final and stops the Russian
crusade. On the other hand, Myskina does not
understand. She won't recover from it. She
even lost the bronze medal to Alicia Molik.
The last thing to know: to whom goes gold
medal? Justine or Amelie?

Because the French did not fail neither. She also made good impression as from the first rounds. Conchita Martinez (6/1, 6/4), Camerin (6/0, 6/1) and Chanda Rubin (6/3, 6/1) may confirm it. Quarterfinals will be even tougher. Her opponent Svetlana Kuznetsova in not unknown anymore. The young 19-year-old Russian hits the ball without doubting. Amelie Mauresmo suffers but she wins the first set. Svetlana does not give up and evens one set for all (6/4). Amelie was feeling the danger and she does not want to leave her Olympic dream fly away: she speeds up and closes the third set more easily 6/2.

Second warning in semi-finals: surprising Alicia Molik, who ousted Sugiyama and Dementieva, showing well-placed and strong serves. Both chose an aggressive game in the first set. Amelie Mauresmo wins it not so easily: 10-8. The most difficult has been done, the second set will be faster: 6/3. The medal is in the French's pocket. Yes, but which medal ? Who will be the Goddess of Athens ? Justine or Amelie ?

The two friends meet the day after on the court. 8,000 people attend their battle. The first games are well-balanced. Amelie Mauresmo leads 3/2, but since the day before, nothing seems to be able to stop the Belgian, who is back at the top of her game. The best of the world. Amelie tries everything, including coming

Virgina Ruano Pascual and Conchita Martinez

to the net, but without success. 6/3, 6/3 in 1.18 hour. "I could not find any solution", the Frenchwoman concludes at the end of the match. She will be happy with silver, while Belgium starts to sing the only 'Brabançonne' (Belgium national anthem) of those Olympic Games in Athens.

Ting Li
and Tian Tian

Women's Doubles

China Wins its First Ever Tennis Gold at Olympics

Emotions in the women's singles tour, where nobody could frighten China. Ting Li and Tian Tian captured gold without any expectation. In final, they defeated the Spanish Conchita Martinez and Virgina Ruano Pascual, top seed No. 2, in two sets (6/3, 6/3). The bronze is for Argentine Suarez and Tarabini. It is the first ever tennis gold medal at Olympics.

Massu Outshines Superstars

A gold medal in singles and another one in doubles tournament. That is what the Chilean brought back to his country from Athens. His doubles team mate Fernando Gonzalez also won a bronze medal in singles. The nation came to Athens having never won any medal in any Olympic sport and went away with three.

In the Men's Singles Race, gold was to be found in South America. Indeed two Chileans came to dig Olympic assets on the European ground. World No. 14 - Nicolas Massu - and World No. 21 - Fernando Gonzalez -. For sure they are two good players but they were far from being announced as favourites before the event. These clay court lovers came and won on hard surface. It was not easy to support for attending champs, who also came to take the rag off the bush. Roger Federer, Andy Roddick, Carlos Moya, Tim Henman, Juan Carlos Ferrero, Marat Safin, among others, were all in Greece. Never before an Olympic Tennis event was so high-levelled, even if Lleyton Hewitt and Andre Agassi did not attend them as they preferred to be ready for the US Open. But all the favourites will make an early exit from the men's singles. The unbeatable Federer will finally be beated. The 18-year-old Czech tennis hope Thomas Berdych proves it as from the second round, when he surprised everybody, ousting the World No. 1. The match is very tough, which confirms the Swiss did not scamp his tournament due to lack of motivation. He is defeated in three sets 6/4, 5/7, 5/7. The other men's tennis 'Hercules', Andy Roddick, has not given up without fighting. If in the second round he managed to win over Tommy Haas with a 9/7 third set, he will be stopped in the third one by Fernando Gonzalez (6/4, 6/4).

On the French side, Gregory Carraz' dreams fly away as from the first round. He is defeated by the former boys' No. 1, Marcos Baghdatis from Cyprus. Arnaud Clement had announced this Olympic Tennis event as his season's main goal. He will win one match. But after having defeated Lapentti, he falls to Croatian Ivo Karlovic, this stadium giant, whose two-meter-high serves were too hard for the 'little'

> "It is just great to be here, so to win two gold medals is simply amazing. Now I can die happy."
>
> *Nicolas Massu,*
> *gold medal in singles*
> *and doubles*

Mardy Fish

Nicolas Massu

Clement. He is ousted in three sets: 7/6, 4/6, 6/4. However, Sebastien Grosjean believed in it. After victories over Horna, Arthurs and Lopez, he faces Fernando Gonzalez in quarterfinals. Due to lack of competition, the French fights for three sets but eventually loses the match (6/2, 2/6, 6/4).

Semifinals will show a duel between USA and Chile: Taylor Dent against Massu (winner over Moya in quarterfinals) and Mardy Fish (winner over Ferrero) against Gonzalez. Four men – Three medals. But all of them want gold. Only one will have it. It won't be Fernando Gonzalez, who will be defeated by Mardy Fish after a nice three-set duel (3/6, 6/3, 6/4). Taylor won't have gold neither. Massu does not give any chance to Dent: 7/6, 6/1. Two matches are still to be played. Two American-Chile duels, both of them ending on a South-American victory.

It is worth to have a look on the final for the bronze medal. The first two sets were not so interesting (1 set for all): the first one for Gonzalez, 6/4, the second for Dent, 6/2. The third one will be tighter. Much tighter. When they started playing it, both players did not think they would play thirty games. At the end of those thirty games, Fernando Gonzalez offers his country its first medal in those Athens Games. Before closing the match after 3.20 hours with a memorable 16/14, he saves two match points. Few hours later, he will save four match points during doubles final.

But Chileans want even more. One more time an American will suffer from it. However, Mardy Fish, Andy Roddick team mate, leads 2 sets against 1. Nicolas Massu seems to be exhausted. He still feels doubles final in his legs. Actually he does not feel his legs at al anymore. He thinks of one single thing: the Olympic title: the second one in less than 48 hours for him. The second one for a country which never had any Olympic medal. He is fighting. He falls several times but he will never give up. In front of him, Fish helps him a bit: he makes 104 unforced faults. Some too much. Massu takes advantage of it and reverses the situation to eventually take the gold medal after exactly four hours playing. In five sets: 6/3, 3/6, 2/6, 6/3, 6/4. This tennis event was incredibly spicy, thanks to Chile.

Taylor Dent

Men's Doubles

Doubles Gold Also Belong to Chile

Three medals, two players, one country: it is the Chilean equation of those Athens Games. Chile captures all its Olympic medals thanks to its two semi-Gods Nicolas Massu and Fernando Gonzalez. Two times in gold for Massu. They share the doubles gold medal. The first gold medal for Chile. The first in 108 years. To get it, both mates went to bed very late. As did the day before Ancic and Ljubicic fighting for bronze medal against Bhupathi and Paes (Croatian victory, with a 16/14 in the third set). It was 01.00 AM. But Chilean did even better. It was 03.00 AM (local time) when they came to the platform. A record. This epic final against the Germans Schuettler and Kiefer had started four hours earlier. And this after 3.5 hours of the match Gonzalez-Dent for the singles

bronze medal. During five sets and 3.40 hours hard game, both were knocking. Nothing to do with the usual tactical shots of doubles matches. In the decisive game of the fourth set, the Germans lead 6 - 2 : 4 match points. But it won't be enough to stop Chile's will to reach this gold medal by any means: 6/2, 4/6, 3/6, 7/6, 6/4. Well done.

Nicolas Massu and Fernando Gonzales

We Can Count on Her

Amelie Mauresmo made it. At the age of 25 years old, she became the fourteenth world No. 1 since 1975, when the computer ranking started. It was her childhood dream that came true. Today she feels stronger, more adult. She is ready to finally capture her first Grand Slam title, which would stop the gossip: the Frenchwoman does not intend to stop now.

"2004 will be Mauresmo's year", Martina Hingis said before the French Open. Apparently, the former world No. 1 was right. The Frenchwoman Amelie Mauresmo probably had the best season of her career. Her self-confidence was very high after a cheering end of the 2003 season (Masters' final, victory with the French team in the Fed Cup) and that helped her to reach quarterfinals quite effortlessly at the Australian Open. She became the world No.3 for the first time in her career. She was feeling pretty well mentally and she thought she could go further but her body did not agree. She had to give up due to a left mid-back muscle strain. She had to stay out of the Tour for two months. As from her comeback in April, she was in the top ten, having won four titles, including three of the greatest titles (after Grand Slams), three Tier I (Berlin, Rome and Montreal, beginning of August). Amelie's results of the 2004 Grand Slam Cup include the semi-finals in Wimbledon and the quarterfinals in the US Open, Roland-Garros and Melbourne. This year, despite all her injuries, she has been the most constant player among her fellow players. Her balance sheet remains positive, but not good enough for a fighter like Amelie, who always wants more. "I want to be world's No. 1", she announced at the Australian Open in 2002. That's a goal, her goal. She has had this idea in mind for more than two years. And this goal has never been as close as it was at this mid-year point. In two years' time, many things happened. Amelie has come a long way. In 2002, she was wondering whether she should give up playing tennis due to a painful knee (cartilage weakness). After having undergone surgery, she was out of the courts for four months and returned only in February 2003. So when the pain came back in January in Melbourne or in Wimbledon's semi-finals (back pain), she lost her confidence. Is Amelie weaker than the others? Maybe, but she is not the only one to be weakened due to the hard rhythm of the WTA Tour.

Physical pain was nothing compared to the grief she felt after her father's death due to cancer in March. Bad luck seemed to be persistent. Amelie bit the bullet. She came out of it much stronger, as

"
I am the world's No. 1 and if you would rather run that down than accept it and be happy for me, go to Hell, that's too bad for you. *"*

Amélie Mauresmo

if those harsh times had made her tougher. "My father's death changed my life forever. Today I have a new strength in me, the events of life helped me grow up. You see things differently, you have other priorities, you deal with people and things in a different way. That's true that I understood better what Justine (Henin-Hardenne), Ferrero and some others felt", she said.

Amelie kept faith, more than ever. She knew that to reach her goal, she had to collect many points. She knew she wouldn't be able to make her dream come true without enormous efforts. Amelie learned from each failure and made the best of them to keep progressing further. She hired a physiotherapist who

> **"** I am really proud to enter History. **"**
>
> *Amélie Mauresmo*

followed her in each tournament to avoid any further physical trouble. So many questions, so many adaptations allowed her to believe that she could do it. She would be world No. 1, one day.

"It would be great but even greater if it came with a major title", she announced in the beginning July. Despite her good ranking, she never captured any major title. Her best Grand Slam result is a final in the Australian Open in 1999. "All of us dream of her being world No. 1", her confident Guy Forget stated, "but between both of awards (Grand Slam winner or world No. 1), the most important is the title, for sure. I think she will capture it. And then, she will be world No. 1, that will be the best of all rewards."

Back from the Olympic Games in Athens with her silver medal, Amelie felt she was getting closer to her goal. Before starting the US Open, pressure was increasing, the famous No. 1 rank was not unreachable anymore. She had to capture the title. "To become world No. 1 through a major title makes the event greater and so it remains in the memories. But the world No. 1, anyway I take it."

Anyway? So much the better. She could not have imagined such a scenario: like in Roland-Garros, Mauresmo failed in quarterfinals against Elena Dementieva. She admitted later that she did not know that in case of a victory against the Russian, she would be sure to climb to the top of the ranking. But it was not over. Amelie still had a chance to get it without making any effort, just waiting for the tournament to go on. Her second chance was to come with the American's defeat in the tournament; it's a matter of mathematics. Moreover, the current No. 1, Justine Henin-Hardenne, had been defeated in the third round.

Friday September 10, at 9.21pm, Svetlana Kuznetsova served her last ace against Lindsay Davenport. The Russian advanced to the US Open final. Some thousands kilometres away from there, watching TV, Amelie Mauresmo understood she had just become world No. 1. She started crying.

Since the creation of the computer ranking, no French had ever reached this rank. Yannick Noah, Cedric Pioline and Nathalie Tauziat never made it pass the third one.

She made it. She reached her goal. Reactions were more or less positive. Backbiters thought very loudly that Mauresmo didn't have too much credit. Indeed Amelie took advantage of the absence of several tough opponents. Kim Clijsters, world No.2 at the beginning of this year, was out of the competition since Indian Wells tournament in March. Since she had many points to defend after her extraordinary 2003 season, the Belgian lost a few ranks. Justine-Henin Hardenne was not top-fit either this year. The virus she got in the beginning of the season kept her from playing in the important events. After the US Open, she was forced to leave the No. 1 she had reached in last November Masters. As for the Williams sisters, they are less frightening than before. They also missed several events due to health troubles. To make a long story short, the toughest opponents of Amelie Mauresmo were not those she was expecting. Since Lindsay Davenport has started thinking about putting

an end to her career, she has captured many victories and many points. After the US Open, she even ended up fighting for the world's first rank with the French. Many Russian players were following them pretty close, ready to climb up to the summit, to challenge Amelie and to remind her that the task was not as easy as it seemed. It is work and not only luck, which led Amelie Mauresmo to achieve her dream. She is the best player on Earth for the time being. "What Amelie has done is just great. It is a pity that those who think she got it thanks to Henin and Clijsters's injuries forget she has also been injured." Mary Pierce, her Fed Cup team-mate, was right. And Guy Forget added: "She took advantage of some favourable circumstances; she has been constant since the beginning of the year, less injured than other ones, so she deserves it. It is a mathematical ranking, so it is not only by chance." Of course others said that it was about time at her age. At the age of 25. And she will replied: "It took me two years and a half to get it. Yeah, it is not so bad, I am not so slow! For sure some were quicker, but some will never get it…" This is also true.

> " We have to give a tribute to Williams sisters, Kim and Justine. They forced us to progress physically to face their domination. They pushed tennis higher. "
>
> *Amélie Mauresmo*

The other thing is that Amelie Mauresmo became world No. 1 without capturing any Grand Slam title, just like Kim Clijsters did. "Nobody can take it back. Those who blame me for not having won a Grand Slam title, I want to tell them: I am the fourteenth player to be world No. 1 since the ranking started (1975). It is not a high number when you compare it to the number of players who won Grand Slam titles in thirty years (thirty of them). Actually it is more difficult to be world No. 1 than to win a Grand Slam!" Lindsay Davenport, her main opponent of the season does not agree: "I have been world No. 1 for a large part of my career but I could only win three Grand Slams!" Amelie got used to mean comments and she won't be diminished by those nasty remarks. It is clear that she would have preferred to win the US Open and therefore to become world No. 1. "It would have been better to reach it that way", she

admitted. "But I know that it is not over and I hope that hearing all people repeating that I did not win any Grand Slam title will push me to go further. Llendl has been world No. 1 before his first major title. I can do the same... " She obviously thinks it is only a step away, one step towards a major title. Of course, she has to work on it. She has to find a solution to her fear in each great event, especially the meeting in Paris in June.

In Roland-Garros, last June, she had to win. It was written in the newspapers and the magazines. She was like paralysed and failed to claim 'her' title, even though her toughest opponents were being defeated one after the other. "The problem with Amelie is that when she is in a Grand Slam, she looks like a girl at Disneyland. She does not realise that she is Minnie, she is on the spot and there is a place for her." Amelie felt too much pressure at home, in front of her audience. "This tournament is what made me to start playing tennis. As it is in France and I am French, I really want to do it well, maybe more than in the other ones. I have to manage that. It is not easy. I have the impression that it is better year after year but there is still something wrong." Amelie still has many doubts about this French Open she needs to overcome. Maybe to win in another Grand Slam tournament would help her to find a solution and come back in Paris with less pressure. Maybe Yannick Noah, her first Fed Cup captain, has a cure for her: "Next year before each match, a coffee-Cognac", he kidded.

Maybe she won't need her captain's pieces of advice to claim the next 2005 great events. Amelie has changed thanks to her new rank. She loosened up, she is more relaxed. She said: "It changes the situation. I loosened up. When you reach the summit, you feel freer; the future can only be happiness. I can think: there is nobody higher than me... This rank increases my desire to go back on the court and work". Especially to go on working with Loic Courteau on small details, which will change everything: change her serve and other small technical problems. Once they will be solved, they will improve her mental condition and give her more confidence in her game. Her coach is optimistic: "One day she will say 'I can do it '. And I would like her to start playing for herself, neither for her father nor for France. She does not have to support the nation's hopes on her shoulders." She will get it, with or without Cognac.

Amelie Mauresmo is the fourteenth World No. 1
(Since creation of computer ranking in 1975)

1 **Chris Evert (USA)** – November 3, 1975, at the age of 20.
2 **Martina Navratilova (TCH-USA)** – July 10, 1978, at the age of 21.
3 **Tracy Austin (USA)** – April 7, 1980, at the age of 17.
4 **Steffi Graf (ALL)** – August 17, 1987, at the age of 17.
5 **Monica Seles (YOU-USA)** – March 11, 1991, at the age of 17.
6 **Arantxa Sanchez (ESP)** – February 6, 1995, at the age of 23.
7 **Martina Hingis (SUI)** – March 31, 1997, at the age of 16.
8 **Lindsay Davenport (USA)** – October 12, 1998, at the age of 21.
9 **Jennifer Capriati (USA)** – October 15, 2001, at the age of 25.
10 **Venus Williams (USA)** – February 25, 2002, at the age of 21.
11 **Serena Williams (USA)** – July 8, 2002, at the age of 20.
12 **Kim Clijsters (BEL)** – August 11, 2003, at the age of 20.
13 **Justine Henin-Hardenne (BEL)** – October 20, 2003, at the age of 21.
14 **Amélie Mauresmo (FRA)** –September 13, 2004, at the age of 25.

Amélie MAURESMO
(Statistics dated from October 18, 2004)

Birthdate: July 5, 1979
Birthplace: Saint-Germain-en-Laye, France
Height: 5'9"
Weight: 142 lbs.
Best ranking: 1 (September 13, 2004)
List of awards: 13 titles

2004	Berlin, Rome, Montreal
2003	Varsovie, Philadelphie
2002	Dubai, Montreal
2001	Paris ('Open Gaz de France'), Nice, Amelia Island, Berlin
2000	Sydney
1999	Bratislava

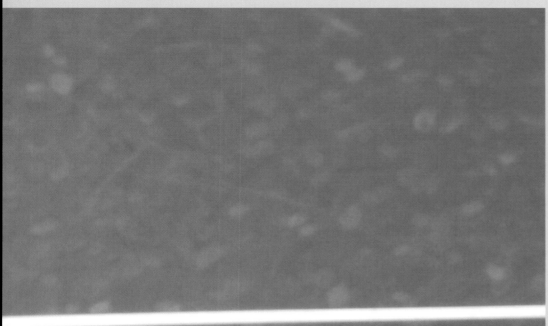

Another Russian Title!

It felt like déjà vu. After Myskina at Roland-Garros and Sharapova at Wimbledon, another Russian captured the last Grand Slam of the year. At Flushing Meadows, Svetlana Kuznetsova won her first great title after defeating her compatriot Elena Dementieva.

Svetlana Kuznetsova

Everybody knows the Russian dolls "matriochki": inside one, there is always another, and then another, and yet another. These dolls could be compared to this year's women tennis and particularly, to the US Open 2004. Indeed, there were fourteen Russians in the last draw. There was still eight of them in the third round, four in the fourth, three in the quarterfinals, two in the semi-finals, and two in the final. Suffice it to say that a Russian eventually won. But as we said, once one is out, there is still another one to replace her.

At the beginning, the top favourites were the winners of the last two Grand Slams. The winner of Roland-Garros first: Anastasia Myskina, Russia's No.1, commander of this Russian army, but she did not meet the expectations. Her disqualification actually was the big surprise of this US Open since she was defeated in the second round. She probably still had not recovered from her incredible defeat in the semi-finals of the Olympic Games against Justine Henin-Hardenne. To make a long story short: she was defeated by the young Chakvetadze, aged 17, Russian. As soon as one had left, another one had already taken her seat. One day, Maria Sharapova would indeed enjoy sitting down in this No.1 seat. But not yet. The Wimbledon winner was indeed not able to repeat her performance in New York. An amazing Mary Pierce defeated her in the third round. Well, a Frenchwoman, this time!

True, there were not only Russians. A lot of American players had come too, to stop the Eastern invasion. There were 23 of them in the first round. Then, in each round, there were as many Russians as Americans up to the semi-finals.

Belgium, for its part, could only count on Justine Henin-Hardenne. Since Kim Clijsters was injured, the new Olympic champion represented the only hope of victory for her country. A country that believed in her, reassured by her performance in Athens. However, Justine informed the Belgian people before the tournament that she was once again feeling tired. In Greece, the efforts had indeed been intense and the virus that had been disturbing her for several months was still there. On the contrary, it kept on bothering her and even spoiled her US Open. In the first round, Justine Henin was not convincing when she played the very young Vaidisova (6/1, 6/4). She dropped one set in the second round against qualified Obziler, an Israeli. Thanks to her determination, she reached the fourth round. She then faced an outstanding Nadia Petrova, ranked fourteenth and of course, Russian.

> "Svetlana was too strong today. There wasn't much I could do. She was too powerful."
>
> *Elena Dementieva*

The title holder was swept away in two short sets: 6/3, 6/2. The word No.1 was no longer No.1 and moreover, this was her last match of the year.

The most coveted rank was then accessible to new candidates. The player who had the best chances to get it was Amelie Mauresmo, the No.1 ... in France. By the way, France is another country where we can find many good women tennis players. The US Open was a good example to illustrate this fact: Mary Pierce reached the fourth round but was defeated by the winner to be. Nathalie Dechy had no choice but to withdraw before the third round where she had to play the finalist to be. Tatiana Golovin (a Frenchwoman with Russian origins) kept on improving. Only Serena Williams was able to stop her in the third round, after a tight match (7/5, 6/4). No substandard performance then for the best "Frenchies". Except maybe for Amelie Mauresmo even though she was the only French player who reached the quarterfinals. One more victory would have enabled her to become the world No.1. A dream. A nightmare as well. The pressure on her prevented her from being completely relaxed during her match against Elena Dementieva. She nevertheless won the first set 6/4. Then, the Russian equalised 4/6. Dementieva gave Mauresmo some opportunities to win the match, especially because of a very bad serve,

but Amelie was not able to take advantage of it and lost the third-set tiebreak. She did not become No.1 yet.

So, Russians and Americans were still competing. Three from each country reached the quarterfinals but there was no match opposing a Russian to an American: Dementieva ousted Mauresmo, Davenport demolished the Japanese Asagoe and the two other matches were 100% Russian and 100% American. In the first, Kuznetsova was stronger than Petrova: 7/6, 6/3. The second was a tense match between two former world No.1 players: Jennifer Capriati facing Serena Williams. The latter showed up in this tournament with a new dress. She had the look of a rebel: leather boots and denim skirt. A rebel that seemed to bother the umpire, Mariana Alves, during this explosive quarterfinal match. One set all, third set: in the first game, Serena smacked a winning backhand. Yes, it was on the line, but on the inside of it. The replays showed it clearly. However, the umpire overruled the linesman's decision: "Advantage Capriati". The match was not over, neither was the discord. Thanks to this break that had been given to her, Capriati served later for the match: 5/4. During this last game, Serena Williams seemed once again to be "betrayed" on three points; this is, in any case, what showed "Hawk Eye", the new computerised graphic

" The US Open is not my favourite tournament, that's for sure: the hubbub, the people talking to each other, the big screen, the music... all this isn't for me. "

Amélie Mauresmo

I Subsequently to Lindsay Davenport's defeat against Kuznetsova, the Frenchwoman Amelie Mauresmo reached for the first time in her career the first place in the world ranking, even though she had been defeated herself in the quarterfinals by Dementieva.

Amélie Mauresmo

Elena Dementieva

O Never in the US Open history had the first four seeds been ousted before the semi-finals. It is only the second time this occurred in a Grand Slam. (Australian Open 1978 and US Open 2004).

system that televisions now have at their disposal. The three points were given to her opponent. This was too much for the rebel for whom the umpiring had no soft spot.

Two Russians. Two Americans. This time, they could not avoid each other: Kuznetsova played Davenport. Capriati was to face Dementieva. Lindsay Davenport was the favourite of the first semi-final. If she had won this US Open, she would have taken back the first place in the world ranking. She had indeed won several successive tournaments and was undefeated since the Wimbledon semi-finals. After Sharapova, Davenport saw another young Russian at the other side of the net: Svetlana Kuznetsova, only 19 but very talented. She hit the ball very hard. However, she had some difficulties to canalise this power in the beginning of the match. The tall American quickly won the first set: 6/1. Kuznetsova hung on. This is one of the numerous things she learned in Spain, in Emilio Sanchez and Sergio Casal's Academy.

And fighting was the right thing to do. The points were getting tighter and in the middle of the second set, Davenport started to make faces. A few games later, the physiotherapist was called on the court and Lindsay Davenport's thigh was bound up. At first, this injury seemed to disturb the young Russian. Too hasty, she forgot to play, to build up the points like she had done so well in the second set she won 6/2. Davenport even led 3/0 in the third set. Kuznetsova woke up right on time to close the match 6/4. The other winner of this match was Amelie Mauresmo who took advantage of the American's defeat to reach the first place in the world ranking. Kuznetsova, for her part, was to play her first Grand Slam final.

Even before the other semi-finals were played, we already knew it would not be the case for her opponent. Capriati had indeed already won in Paris and Melbourne and Dementieva has already reached a final at Roland-Garros this year. The two players wanted to make their dream come true: Capriati wanted to win in New York, at last, and Dementieva wanted to capture her first great title. Both determined, the two players played the most thrilling match of the tournament. One year before, Capriati failed at the same stage of the competition, on the same court. The court Arthur Ashe still remembered her epic duel against Justine Henin-Hardenne in 2003. And History repeated itself. Capriati was defeated in the third set tiebreak of the semi-finals, even though she held on tight, just as when she played Monica Seles in 1991 or Justine Henin-Hardenne in 2003. In the first set, Dementieva was untouchable and hit a whole string of winners against Capriati, who was helpless: 6/0. In the second set, the Russian lost her focus, just as Serena did in the quarterfinals. This was a mistake not to be made in front of a player such as Capriati, who reversed the situation and equalised: "one set all". The third set was splendid. Capriati even served for the match, to eventually reach this final that did not seem to want her. This was once again the case. Dementieva won the tiebreak 7 to 5. Once again, no American would play the final. Two Russians were to face each other on Saturday.

The final was less exciting than the semi-finals. Elena Dementieva was the only player to reach two Grand Slam finals this year, but without winning any. Once again, she let this great opportunity slip through her hands. Svetlana Kuznetsova played a sound match and captured it with no surprise 6/3, 7/5. She also was the third Russian to win a Grand Slam this year. Who's next? Elena Dementieva is waiting for her turn, as patient as a doll. After the final, which was played on September 11, she said she was thinking of the American victims of 2001 and of the Russian victims of the Beslan slaughter, which occurred a few days only before this final. The Americans and the Russians, two peoples opposing each other in this competition but united in the same grief.

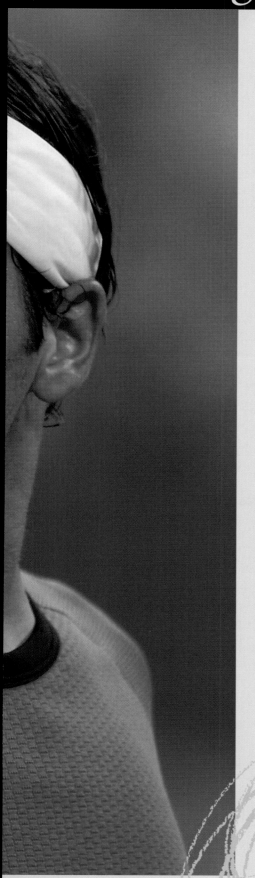

Three out of Four!

This is called a Small Slam. Roger Federer captured his third Grand Slam title this year at Flushing Meadows. Nothing and nobody, not even Lleyton Hewitt in the final, could stop the world No. 1.

Both world No.1 and No. 2 were expected in the final but only one of them made it. The Americans did not get the final they dreamed of. Andy Roddick could not join Roger Federer in the US Open final. And the one to blame is the 22-year-old Swede Joachim Johansson. Tall and strong, he beat the American with the same qualities: huge serves and violent forehands.

The battle took place on Thursday September 8, in night session. Andy was the top favourite of these quarterfinals. However, the Swede was surprising and won the first two sets: 6/4, 6/4. Two break points were enough for him to sail away. The match was interrupted due to rain and then, the American came back to show his rage to win. He evened to two sets all (6/3, 6/2). That night in New York, Arthur Ashe court's audience woke up. Roddick seemed unbeatable. 4/4 in this decisive set and he had a break point. His passing shot was out. His last chance just fade away. It's the young Swede's turn to be lucky in the next game. Johansson broke Roddick for the third time in the match. The one game Johansson shouldn't have broken for Roddick to win. The defending champ was out. The world No. 2 left Flushing Meadows. This happened to the top seed No. 3 Carlos Moya three days earlier. The Spanish was defeated by the Belgian Olivier Rochus, world No. 100.

Who would be able to stop Roger Federer? Albert Costa (7/5, 6/2, 6/4), Marcos Baghdatis (6/2, 6/7, 6/3, 6/1) and Fabrice Santoro could hardly worry him. Andrei Pavel, injured in the back, didn't even come on the court to meet the Swiss in the third round. Federer was frightening but Andre Agassi has already met other worrisome opponents. Indeed, he has defeated great players in his career. So he is impatient to meet Roger. In quarterfinals, the first three sets were final-worthy: 6/3, 2/6,

> " It seems to me that once you win in New York, you may win anything, anywhere. "
>
> *Roger Federer*

Tommy
Haas

7/5. Federer lead two sets against one, but Agassi, who returned the ball very quickly, put him in trouble. The best is still to come. Both opponents started playing at a higher level. Rain stopped their eagerness. The next day, the weather was too windy for them to shine. Squalls made magic shots impossible, even for the two best players on Earth. In the fourth set, Roger Federer made four double faults in his serve game. This break was enough for Andre Agassi: two sets all. The situation was reversed over and over again. Indeed, Roger Federer managed to fly away in the last set: 6/3. The Swiss could control all the elements. What happened next in the tournament proved that Federer is at ease on a court.

Let us start with the semi-finals where the Swiss met Tim Henman, his Pet Peeve. The British won six matches and the Swiss two out of the eight matches they played against each other. For the second time of the year, Henman reached semis in a Grand Slam, after Roland-Garros. Like in Paris, the British did not hesitate to play overtime: three five-set matches, only two matches in four sets. At the age of 30, Henman is still running after his first Grand Slam title. He is still running because Federer is better. In three sets, the Swiss reminded his Pet Peeve who was the world No. 1. He did not pay attention to the statistics. After all he had never been in the last 16 in New York before this time. Roger prefers to look at records, to beat them. No player has ever won his first four Grand Slam finals. The first three were already in his pocket (two Wimbledon and one the Australian Open). Who would be on the other side of the net for fourth? World No. 2 (Roddick), 3 (Moya), 5 (Henman) and 6 (Agassi) left. Only world No. 4 was remaining: Lleyton Hewitt. That was not a surprise. The Australian was top-fit again. He

I It is the 1st time a Cypriot wins a match in the main draw of a grand-slam event. The 19-year-old Marcos Baghdatis had the honour to beat Frenchman Olivier Mutis and to face the winner-to-be Roger Federer of the second round.

Joachim Johansson and Andy Roddick

The US Open's Sleeper

His name is Joachim Johannsson

He ousted the defending champion Andy Roddick in quarterfinals. Then he was defeated by his brother-in-law-to-be Lleyton Hewitt. He is the boyfriend of Jaslyn, the Australian's sister. He is 22 years old. He is tall (6'6", 198 lbs). He served 106 aces at the US Open, the record of the tournament. His father played in the Davis Cup team in 1974. He was born in the same city as Björn Borg, in Sodertalje. He is thus Swedish. His nickname is Pim-Pim. He will be on people's mind for a long time. Actually his name is Joachim Johannsson!

felt as well as in 2001, when he won the final here. His good shape allowed him to win Long Island and Washington just before the US open. The first rounds confirm that Lleyton found his career best form. As John Newcombe (Davis Cup Australian captain) says, "Lleyton has now the look of a hunter. Last year he had the look of the game." A hunter, with an impressive quickness: six victories. He captured the first one against a dinosaur: Wayne Ferreira, the man who won 59 Grand Slam titles in a row - a record. Ferreira will certainly have plenty of nice stories to tell his grandchildren although his last Grand Slam is probably not his best. The "Aussie" overwhelmed him. The South-African played his last three sets and left the court for the last time. Respect. Lleyton Hewitt went on in his ascension to the top, without meeting any obstacle. Arazi, Lopez, Beck and Tommy Haas didn't worry him, neither did Ferreira. He didn't lose one single set against those guys.

The Australian reached semi-finals where he played Joachim Johansson. Both men know each other quite well. Joachim is the boyfriend of Jaslyn, Lleyton's sister, and both players are used to train together during the winter in Adelaide. But this time, it won't be a family match or a friends' party. It is a Grand Slam semi-final match, the first for Johansson. And it was obvious. Lleyton Hewitt's experience made the difference: no pity for the "little" (6'6", 198 lbs.) brother-in-law. The Australian didn't find himself

in trouble very often and he won once again in three sets: 6/4, 7/5, 6/3. Joachim could join Jaslyn in the audience. Lleyton joins Roger on the court, Arthur Ashe's court, where more than 20,000 people attended the final.

Everybody thought it would be a great battle: huge talent on one side and unique willpower on the other, the perfect match when it comes to suspense and emotion. The problem was that on that Sunday, September 12, Roger Federer was an alien. After 18 minutes (6/0), the whole tennis planet was convinced. Lleyton Hewitt the first. He was totally paralysed during last three games of the first set: three love games, twelve winners in a row. In a Grand Slam final! Never before had a serve seemed as easy to play, a backhand as fluid and a forehand as simple. Broken in the first game of the second set, Lleyton Hewitt could not catch up. But he was not knocked-out yet. The Australian fighter tried to come back into the match. He evened 2/2. Federer speeded up the process: 4/2, 0-40 on Lleyton Hewitt's serve. He could have given up. But he did not, not yet. He came back and even if Federer was serving for the set (5/4), Hewitt saved two set points, coming to a tie break. Is it enough to give some doubts to the Swiss? Not really. On that day Federer did exactly what he wanted. He captured the first four points of this decisive game and concluded (7-3): two sets - zero. This time Lleyton Hewitt had to come back to reality: Federer was stronger. The Australian understood his high fighting spirit wouldn't be sufficient against this Federer. He was unbeatable. The third set came to an end as quickly as the first: 6/0, 7/6, 6/0. 1.51 hour of a unique one-way game.

Roger Federer joins the greats. We had no doubt about it. He became the first player since Mats Wilander in 1988 to win three Grand Slam titles the same year: a small Slam, waiting for the Grand. To anyone who would be interested, Roger Federer is still looking for a coach.

56

The South-African Wayne Ferreira broke a record. He played his 56th tournament in a row at the US Open. For his last match he was defeated in the first round by the finalist Lleyton Hewitt.

US OPEN

| 1st round | 2nd round | 3rd round | 4th round | Quarterfinals | Semifinals |

1st round / 2nd round / 3rd round / 4th round / Quarterfinals / Semifinals

- 1 J. HENIN (B) — J. HENIN
- Q N. VAIDISOVA (CZ) — 6-1 6-4 — J. HENIN 6-2 5-7 6-2
- Q T. OBZILER (IL) — T. OBZILER
- Q A. WIDJAJA (IND) — 7-5 6-3 — J. HENIN 6-4 6-3
- A. JIDKOVA (RUS) — L. RAYMOND
- L. RAYMOND (USA) — 7-5 6-3 — L. RAYMOND 4-6 7-6(3) 6-2
- M. KIRILENKO (RUS) — M. KIRILENKO
- 25 E. LIKHOVTSEVA (RUS) — 7-6(3) 6-3
- 19 S. FARINA ELIA (I) — S. FARINA ELIA
- Q A. SPEARS (USA) — 3-6 6-2 6-4 — S. FARINA ELIA 6-2 6-1
- T. PANOVA (RUS) — K. SREBOTNIK
- K. SREBOTNIK (SLO) — 6-3 6-2 — N. PETROVA 4-6 7-6(6) 7-6(3)
- S. STOSUR (AUS) — S. STOSUR
- V. RAZZANO (F) — 7-5 6-4 — N. PETROVA 6-2 6-2
- J. ZHENG (RCH) — N. PETROVA
- 14 N. PETROVA (RUS) — 6-0 6-1 — N. PETROVA 6-3 6-2
- 9 S. KUZNETSOVA (RUS) — S. KUZNETSOVA
- Q S. KARATANCHEVA (BG) — 6-2 6-0 — S. KUZNETSOVA 6-3 6-3
- C. CASTANO (COL) — N. PRATT
- N. PRATT (AUS) — 3-6 6-1 6-3 — S. KUZNETSOVA 7-6(3) 7-5
- M. SEQUERA (YU) — K. BRANDI
- K. BRANDI (PUR) — 6-1 6-2 — A. FRAZIER 6-4 6-1
- K. MC CAIN (USA) — A. FRAZIER
- 21 A. FRAZIER (USA) — 6-2 6-2 — S. KUZNETSOVA 7-6(5) 6-2
- 27 M. PIERCE (F) — M. PIERCE
- E. LOIT (F) — 6-1 6-2 — M. PIERCE 6-0 6-1
- A. STEVENSON (USA) — V. RUANO PASCUAL
- V. RUANO PASCUAL (E) — 6-4 7-5 — M. PIERCE 4-6 6-2 6-3
- J. JANKOVIC (YU) — J. JANKOVIC
- Q N. LLAGOSTERA VI. (E) — 6-3 6-4 — M. SHARAPOVA 6-0 6-7(5) 6-1
- L. GRANVILLE (USA) — M. SHARAPOVA
- 7 M. SHARAPOVA (RUS) — 6-3 5-7 7-5
- 4 A. MYSKINA (RUS) — A. MYSKINA
- L. CERVANOVA (SK) — 6-1 6-0 — A. CHAKVETADZE 7-6(3) 6-3
- B. SCHETT (A) — A. CHAKVETADZE
- Q A. CHAKVETADZE (RUS) — 1-6 6-4 6-2 — E. DANIILIDOU 6-4 6-2
- B. STRYCOVA (CZ) — A. MEDINA GARRIG.
- A. MEDINA GARRIG. (E) — 7-5 6-3 — E. DANIILIDOU 1-6 7-5 6-4
- S. TALAJA (CRO) — E. DANIILIDOU
- 29 E. DANIILIDOU (GR) — 3-6 6-3 7-5
- 24 A. SMASHNOVA-PIS. (IL) — S. ASAGOE
- S. ASAGOE (J) — 3-6 6-4 6-1 — S. ASAGOE 7-5 6-3
- T. PISNIK (SLO) — J. CRAYBAS
- J. CRAYBAS (USA) — 6-2 6-1 — S. ASAGOE 6-4 6-4
- D. RANDRIANTEFY (MA) — D. RANDRIANTEFY
- J. KIRKLAND (USA) — 6-4 6-4 — P. SUAREZ 6-2 6-2
- Q N. LIU (RCH) — P. SUAREZ
- 13 P. SUAREZ (ARG) — 6-1 7-5
- 11 V. WILLIAMS (USA) — V. WILLIAMS
- P. MANDULA (H) — 6-3 7-6(3) — V. WILLIAMS 7-5 6-1
- S. OBATA (J) — S. UBEROI
- Q S. UBEROI (USA) — 6-3 3-6 7-5 — V. WILLIAMS 7-6(4) 6-3
- Q A. SERRA ZANETTI (I) — A. SERRA ZANETTI
- M. WASHINGTON (USA) — 7-5 7-5 — C. RUBIN 7-5 6-3
- M. SANCHEZ LOREN. (E) — C. RUBIN
- 20 C. RUBIN (USA) — 6-2 6-2
- 26 E. BOVINA (RUS) — E. BOVINA
- M. MARRERO (E) — 6-3 6-0 — E. BOVINA 6-2 7-5
- M. CAMERIN (I) — M. CAMERIN
- M. CZINK (H) — 6-4 6-2 — L. DAVENPORT 7-6(7) 6-1
- A. PARRA (E) — A. PARRA
- M. WEINGARTNER (D) — 6-2 7-6(5) — L. DAVENPORT 6-4 6-2
- L. KURHAJCOVA (SK) — L. DAVENPORT
- 5 L. DAVENPORT (USA) — 6-4 6-0

Quarterfinals / Semifinals:
- J. HENIN — N. PETROVA 6-3 6-2
- S. KUZNETSOVA 7-6(3) 7-5
- E. DANIILIDOU — S. ASAGOE 7-6(4) 4-6 6-3
- V. WILLIAMS — L. DAVENPORT 7-5 6-4

Semifinals:
- N. PETROVA — S. KUZNETSOVA 7-6(4) 6-3
- S. ASAGOE — L. DAVENPORT 6-1 6-1

Final:
- S. KUZNETSOVA 1-6 6-2 6-4

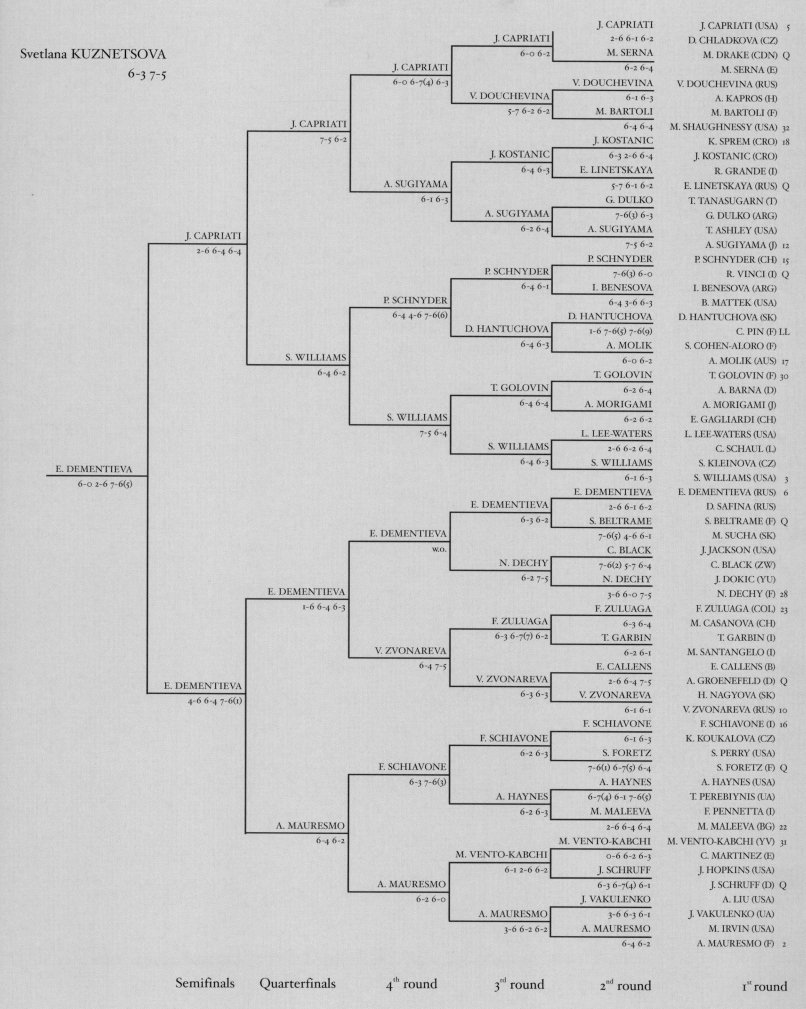

Svetlana KUZNETSOVA
6-3 7-5

E. DEMENTIEVA
6-0 2-6 7-6(5)

J. CAPRIATI
2-6 6-4 6-4

E. DEMENTIEVA
4-6 6-4 7-6(1)

J. CAPRIATI
7-5 6-2

S. WILLIAMS
6-4 6-2

E. DEMENTIEVA
1-6 6-4 6-3

A. MAURESMO
6-4 6-2

J. CAPRIATI
6-0 6-7(4) 6-3

A. SUGIYAMA
6-1 6-3

P. SCHNYDER
6-4 4-6 7-6(6)

S. WILLIAMS
7-5 6-4

E. DEMENTIEVA
w.o.

V. ZVONAREVA
6-4 7-5

F. SCHIAVONE
6-3 7-6(3)

A. MAURESMO
6-2 6-0

J. CAPRIATI
6-0 6-2

V. DOUCHEVINA
5-7 6-2 6-2

J. KOSTANIC
6-4 6-3

A. SUGIYAMA
6-2 6-4

P. SCHNYDER
6-4 6-1

D. HANTUCHOVA
6-4 6-3

T. GOLOVIN
6-4 6-4

S. WILLIAMS
6-4 6-3

E. DEMENTIEVA
6-3 6-2

N. DECHY
6-2 7-5

F. ZULUAGA
6-3 6-7(7) 6-2

V. ZVONAREVA
6-3 6-3

F. SCHIAVONE
6-2 6-3

A. HAYNES
6-2 6-3

M. VENTO-KABCHI
6-1 2-6 6-2

A. MAURESMO
3-6 6-2 6-2

J. CAPRIATI
2-6 6-1 6-2

M. SERNA
6-2 6-4

V. DOUCHEVINA
6-1 6-3

M. BARTOLI
6-4 6-4

J. KOSTANIC
6-3 2-6 6-4

E. LINETSKAYA
5-7 6-1 6-2

G. DULKO
7-6(3) 6-3

A. SUGIYAMA
7-5 6-2

P. SCHNYDER
7-6(3) 6-0

I. BENESOVA
6-4 3-6 6-3

D. HANTUCHOVA
1-6 7-6(5) 7-6(9)

A. MOLIK
6-0 6-2

T. GOLOVIN
6-2 6-4

A. MORIGAMI
6-2 6-2

L. LEE-WATERS
2-6 6-2 6-4

S. WILLIAMS
6-1 6-3

E. DEMENTIEVA
2-6 6-1 6-2

S. BELTRAME
7-6(5) 4-6 6-1

C. BLACK
7-6(2) 5-7 6-4

N. DECHY
3-6 6-0 7-5

F. ZULUAGA
6-3 6-4

T. GARBIN
6-2 6-1

E. CALLENS
2-6 6-4 7-5

V. ZVONAREVA
6-1 6-1

F. SCHIAVONE
6-1 6-3

S. FORETZ
7-6(1) 6-7(5) 6-4

A. HAYNES
6-7(4) 6-1 7-6(5)

M. MALEEVA
2-6 6-4 6-4

M. VENTO-KABCHI
0-6 6-2 6-3

J. SCHRUFF
6-3 6-7(4) 6-1

J. VAKULENKO
3-6 6-3 6-1

A. MAURESMO
6-4 6-2

J. CAPRIATI (USA)   5
D. CHLADKOVA (CZ)
M. DRAKE (CDN)   Q
M. SERNA (E)
V. DOUCHEVINA (RUS)
A. KAPROS (H)
M. BARTOLI (F)
M. SHAUGHNESSY (USA)   32
K. SPREM (CRO)   18
J. KOSTANIC (CRO)
R. GRANDE (I)
E. LINETSKAYA (RUS)   Q
T. TANASUGARN (T)
G. DULKO (ARG)
T. ASHLEY (USA)
A. SUGIYAMA (J)   12
P. SCHNYDER (CH)   15
R. VINCI (I)   Q
I. BENESOVA (ARG)
B. MATTEK (USA)
D. HANTUCHOVA (SK)
C. PIN (F) LL
S. COHEN-ALORO (F)
A. MOLIK (AUS)   17
T. GOLOVIN (F)   30
A. BARNA (D)
A. MORIGAMI (J)
E. GAGLIARDI (CH)
L. LEE-WATERS (USA)
C. SCHAUL (L)
S. KLEINOVA (CZ)
S. WILLIAMS (USA)   3
E. DEMENTIEVA (RUS)   6
D. SAFINA (RUS)
S. BELTRAME (F)   Q
M. SUCHA (SK)
J. JACKSON (USA)
C. BLACK (ZW)
J. DOKIC (YU)
N. DECHY (F)   28
F. ZULUAGA (COL)   23
M. CASANOVA (CH)
T. GARBIN (I)
M. SANTANGELO (I)
E. CALLENS (B)
A. GROENEFELD (D)   Q
H. NAGYOVA (SK)
V. ZVONAREVA (RUS)   10
F. SCHIAVONE (I)   16
K. KOUKALOVA (CZ)
S. PERRY (USA)
S. FORETZ (F)   Q
A. HAYNES (USA)
T. PEREBIYNIS (UA)
F. PENNETTA (I)
M. MALEEVA (BG)   22
M. VENTO-KABCHI (YV)   31
C. MARTINEZ (E)
J. HOPKINS (USA)
J. SCHRUFF (D)   Q
A. LIU (USA)
J. VAKULENKO (UA)
M. IRVIN (USA)
A. MAURESMO (F)   2

Semifinals   Quarterfinals   4th round   3rd round   2nd round   1st round

*walkover

US Open

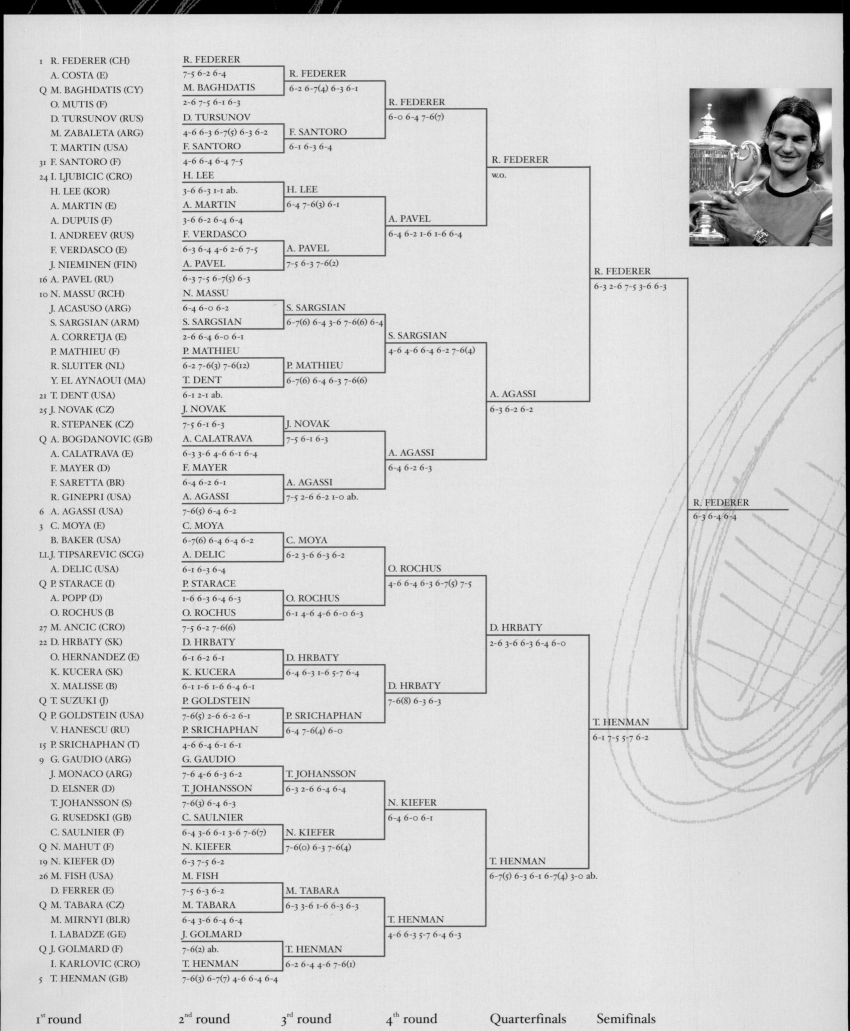

| 1st round | 2nd round | 3rd round | 4th round | Quarterfinals | Semifinals |

1 R. FEDERER (CH)
A. COSTA (E)
Q M. BAGHDATIS (CY)
O. MUTIS (F)
D. TURSUNOV (RUS)
M. ZABALETA (ARG)
T. MARTIN (USA)
31 F. SANTORO (F)
24 I. LJUBICIC (CRO)
H. LEE (KOR)
A. MARTIN (E)
A. DUPUIS (F)
I. ANDREEV (RUS)
F. VERDASCO (E)
J. NIEMINEN (FIN)
16 A. PAVEL (RU)
10 N. MASSU (RCH)
J. ACASUSO (ARG)
S. SARGSIAN (ARM)
A. CORRETJA (E)
P. MATHIEU (F)
R. SLUITER (NL)
Y. EL AYNAOUI (MA)
21 T. DENT (USA)
25 J. NOVAK (CZ)
R. STEPANEK (CZ)
Q A. BOGDANOVIC (GB)
A. CALATRAVA (E)
F. MAYER (D)
F. SARETTA (BR)
R. GINEPRI (USA)
6 A. AGASSI (USA)
3 C. MOYA (E)
B. BAKER (USA)
LL J. TIPSAREVIC (SCG)
A. DELIC (USA)
Q P. STARACE (I)
A. POPP (D)
O. ROCHUS (B)
27 M. ANCIC (CRO)
22 D. HRBATY (SK)
O. HERNANDEZ (E)
K. KUCERA (SK)
X. MALISSE (B)
Q T. SUZUKI (J)
Q P. GOLDSTEIN (USA)
V. HANESCU (RU)
15 P. SRICHAPHAN (T)
9 G. GAUDIO (ARG)
J. MONACO (ARG)
D. ELSNER (D)
T. JOHANSSON (S)
G. RUSEDSKI (GB)
C. SAULNIER (F)
Q N. MAHUT (F)
19 N. KIEFER (D)
26 M. FISH (USA)
D. FERRER (E)
Q M. TABARA (CZ)
M. MIRNYI (BLR)
I. LABADZE (GE)
Q J. GOLMARD (F)
I. KARLOVIC (CRO)
5 T. HENMAN (GB)

1st round / 2nd round

R. FEDERER
7-5 6-2 6-4

M. BAGHDATIS
2-6 7-5 6-1 6-3

D. TURSUNOV
4-6 6-3 6-7(5) 6-3 6-2

F. SANTORO
4-6 6-4 6-4 7-5

H. LEE
3-6 6-3 1-1 ab.

A. MARTIN
3-6 6-2 6-4 6-4

F. VERDASCO
6-3 6-4 4-6 2-6 7-5

A. PAVEL
6-3 7-5 6-7(5) 6-3

N. MASSU
6-4 6-0 6-2

S. SARGSIAN
2-6 6-4 6-0 6-1

P. MATHIEU
6-2 7-6(3) 7-6(12)

T. DENT
6-1 2-1 ab.

J. NOVAK
7-5 6-1 6-3

A. CALATRAVA
6-3 3-6 4-6 6-1 6-4

F. MAYER
6-4 6-2 6-1

A. AGASSI
7-6(5) 6-4 6-2

C. MOYA
6-7(6) 6-4 6-4 6-2

A. DELIC
6-1 6-3 6-4

P. STARACE
1-6 6-3 6-4 6-3

O. ROCHUS
7-5 6-2 7-6(6)

D. HRBATY
6-1 6-2 6-1

K. KUCERA
6-1 1-6 1-6 6-4 6-1

P. GOLDSTEIN
7-6(5) 2-6 6-2 6-1

P. SRICHAPHAN
4-6 6-4 6-1 6-1

G. GAUDIO
7-6 4-6 6-3 6-2

T. JOHANSSON
7-6(3) 6-4 6-3

C. SAULNIER
6-4 3-6 6-1 3-6 7-6(7)

N. KIEFER
6-3 7-5 6-2

M. FISH
7-5 6-3 6-2

M. TABARA
6-4 3-6 6-4 6-4

J. GOLMARD
7-6(2) ab.

T. HENMAN
7-6(3) 6-7(7) 4-6 6-4 6-4

2nd round

R. FEDERER
6-2 6-7(4) 6-3 6-1

F. SANTORO
6-1 6-3 6-4

H. LEE
6-4 7-6(3) 6-1

A. PAVEL
7-5 6-3 7-6(2)

S. SARGSIAN
6-7(6) 6-4 3-6 7-6(6) 6-4

P. MATHIEU
6-7(6) 6-4 6-3 7-6(6)

J. NOVAK
7-5 6-1 6-3

A. AGASSI
7-5 2-6 6-2 1-0 ab.

C. MOYA
6-2 3-6 6-3 6-2

O. ROCHUS
6-1 4-6 4-6 6-0 6-3

D. HRBATY
6-4 6-3 1-6 5-7 6-4

P. SRICHAPHAN
6-4 7-6(4) 6-0

T. JOHANSSON
6-3 2-6 6-4 6-4

N. KIEFER
7-6(0) 6-3 7-6(4)

M. TABARA
6-3 3-6 1-6 6-3 6-3

T. HENMAN
6-2 6-4 4-6 7-6(1)

3rd round

R. FEDERER
6-0 6-4 7-6(7)

A. PAVEL
6-4 6-2 1-6 1-6 6-4

S. SARGSIAN
4-6 4-6 6-4 6-2 7-6(4)

A. AGASSI
6-4 6-2 6-3

C. MOYA
6-2 3-6 6-3 6-2

D. HRBATY
7-6(8) 6-3 6-3

N. KIEFER
6-4 6-0 6-1

T. HENMAN
4-6 6-3 5-7 6-4 6-3

4th round

R. FEDERER
w.o.

A. AGASSI
6-3 6-2 6-2

O. ROCHUS
4-6 6-4 6-3 6-7(5) 7-5

D. HRBATY
2-6 3-6 6-3 6-4 6-0

Quarterfinals

R. FEDERER
6-3 2-6 7-5 3-6 6-3

T. HENMAN
6-1 7-5 5-7 6-2

Semifinals

R. FEDERER
6-1 7-5 5-7 6-2

Final

R. FEDERER
6-3 6-4 6-4

T. HENMAN
6-7(5) 6-3 6-1 6-7(4) 3-0 ab.

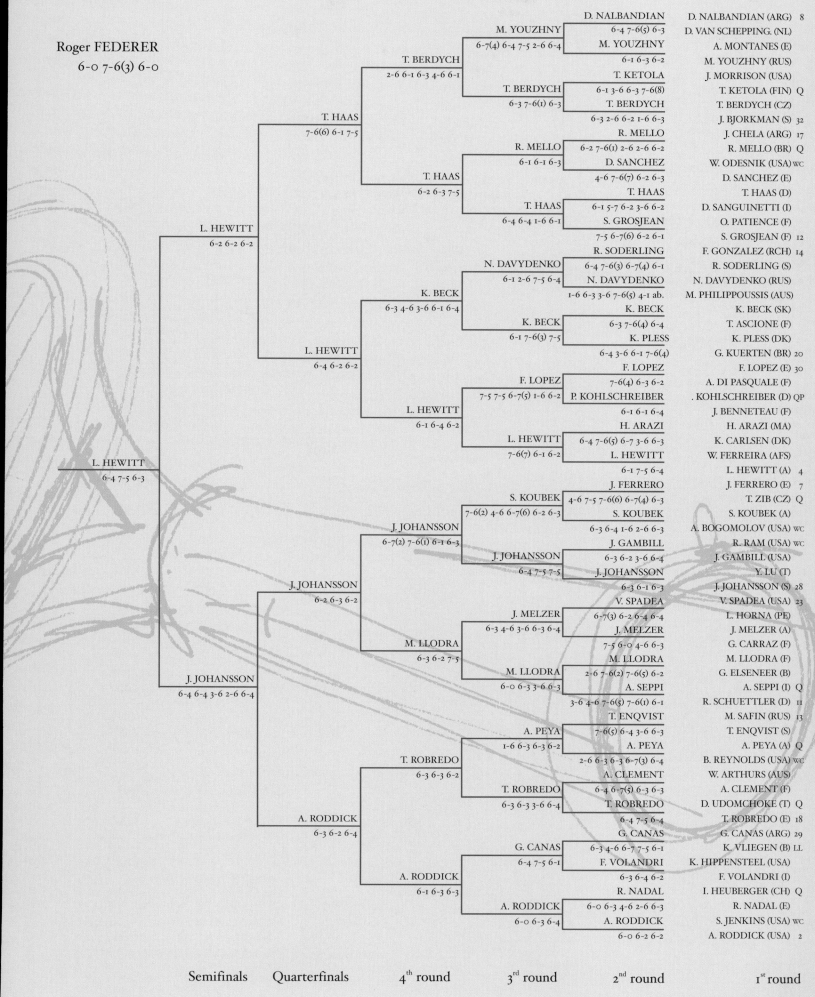

Roger FEDERER

6-0 7-6(3) 6-0

				D. NALBANDIAN		D. NALBANDIAN (ARG)	8
			M. YOUZHNY	6-4 7-6(5) 6-3		D. VAN SCHEPPING. (NL)	
			6-7(4) 6-4 7-5 2-6 6-4	M. YOUZHNY		A. MONTANES (E)	
		T. BERDYCH		6-1 6-3 6-2		M. YOUZHNY (RUS)	
		2-6 6-1 6-3 4-6 6-1	T. KETOLA			J. MORRISON (USA)	
			T. BERDYCH	6-1 3-6 6-3 7-6(8)		T. KETOLA (FIN)	Q
			6-3 7-6(1) 6-3	T. BERDYCH		T. BERDYCH (CZ)	
	T. HAAS			6-3 2-6 6-2 1-6 6-3		J. BJORKMAN (S)	32
	7-6(6) 6-1 7-5			R. MELLO		J. CHELA (ARG)	17
			R. MELLO	6-2 7-6(1) 2-6 2-6 6-2		R. MELLO (BR)	Q
			6-1 6-1 6-3	D. SANCHEZ		W. ODESNIK (USA)	WC
		T. HAAS		4-6 7-6(7) 6-2 6-3		D. SANCHEZ (E)	
		6-2 6-3 7-5	T. HAAS			T. HAAS (D)	
			T. HAAS	6-1 5-7 6-2 3-6 6-2		D. SANGUINETTI (I)	
			6-4 6-4 1-6 6-1	S. GROSJEAN		O. PATIENCE (F)	
L. HEWITT				7-5 6-7(6) 6-2 6-1		S. GROSJEAN (F)	12
6-2 6-2 6-2				R. SODERLING		F. GONZALEZ (RCH)	14
			N. DAVYDENKO	6-4 7-6(3) 6-7(4) 6-1		R. SODERLING (S)	
			6-1 2-6 7-5 6-4	N. DAVYDENKO		N. DAVYDENKO (RUS)	
		K. BECK		1-6 6-3 3-6 7-6(5) 4-1 ab.		M. PHILIPPOUSSIS (AUS)	
		6-3 4-6 3-6 6-1 6-4	K. BECK			K. BECK (SK)	
			K. BECK	6-3 7-6(4) 6-4		T. ASCIONE (F)	
			6-1 7-6(3) 7-5	K. PLESS		K. PLESS (DK)	
	L. HEWITT			6-4 3-6 6-1 7-6(4)		G. KUERTEN (BR)	20
	6-4 6-2 6-2			F. LOPEZ		F. LOPEZ (E)	30
			F. LOPEZ	7-6(4) 6-3 6-2		A. DI PASQUALE (F)	
			7-5 7-5 6-7(5) 1-6 6-2	P. KOHLSCHREIBER		. KOHLSCHREIBER (D)	QP
		L. HEWITT		6-1 6-1 6-4		J. BENNETEAU (F)	
		6-1 6-4 6-2	H. ARAZI			H. ARAZI (MA)	
			L. HEWITT	6-4 7-6(5) 6-7 3-6 6-3		K. CARLSEN (DK)	
			7-6(7) 6-1 6-2	L. HEWITT		W. FERREIRA (AFS)	
L. HEWITT				6-1 7-5 6-4		L. HEWITT (A)	4
6-4 7-5 6-3				J. FERRERO		J. FERRERO (E)	7
			S. KOUBEK	4-6 7-5 7-6(6) 6-7(4) 6-3		T. ZIB (CZ)	Q
			7-6(2) 4-6 6-7(6) 6-2 6-3	S. KOUBEK		S. KOUBEK (A)	
		J. JOHANSSON		6-3 6-4 1-6 2-6 6-3		A. BOGOMOLOV (USA)	WC
		6-7(2) 7-6(1) 6-1 6-3	J. GAMBILL			R. RAM (USA)	WC
			J. JOHANSSON	6-3 6-2 3-6 6-4		J. GAMBILL (USA)	
			6-4 7-5 7-5	J. JOHANSSON		Y. LU (T)	
	J. JOHANSSON			6-3 6-1 6-3		J. JOHANSSON (S)	28
	6-2 6-3 6-2			V. SPADEA		V. SPADEA (USA)	23
			J. MELZER	6-7(3) 6-2 6-4 6-4		L. HORNA (PE)	
			6-3 4-6 3-6 6-3 6-4	J. MELZER		J. MELZER (A)	
		M. LLODRA		7-5 6-0 4-6 6-3		G. CARRAZ (F)	
		6-3 6-2 7-5	M. LLODRA			M. LLODRA (F)	
			M. LLODRA	2-6 7-6(2) 7-6(5) 6-2		G. ELSENEER (B)	
			6-0 6-3 3-6 6-3	A. SEPPI		A. SEPPI (I)	Q
J. JOHANSSON				3-6 4-6 7-6(5) 7-6(1) 6-1		R. SCHUETTLER (D)	11
6-4 6-4 3-6 2-6 6-4				T. ENQVIST		M. SAFIN (RUS)	13
			A. PEYA	7-6(5) 6-4 3-6 6-3		T. ENQVIST (S)	
			1-6 6-3 6-3 6-2	A. PEYA		A. PEYA (A)	Q
		T. ROBREDO		2-6 6-3 6-3 6-7(3) 6-4		B. REYNOLDS (USA)	WC
		6-3 6-3 6-2	A. CLEMENT			W. ARTHURS (AUS)	
			T. ROBREDO	6-4 6-7(5) 6-3 6-3		A. CLEMENT (F)	
			6-3 6-3 3-6 6-4	T. ROBREDO		D. UDOMCHOKE (T)	Q
	A. RODDICK			6-4 7-5 6-4		T. ROBREDO (E)	18
	6-3 6-2 6-4			G. CANAS		G. CANAS (ARG)	29
			G. CANAS	6-3 4-6 6-7 7-5 6-1		K. VLIEGEN (B)	LL
			6-4 7-5 6-1	F. VOLANDRI		K. HIPPENSTEEL (USA)	
		A. RODDICK		6-3 6-4 6-2		F. VOLANDRI (I)	
		6-1 6-3 6-3	R. NADAL			I. HEUBERGER (CH)	Q
			A. RODDICK	6-0 6-3 4-6 2-6 6-3		R. NADAL (E)	
			6-0 6-3 6-4	A. RODDICK		S. JENKINS (USA)	WC
				6-0 6-2 6-2		A. RODDICK (USA)	2

*walkover

The Finalists (statistics on September 13, 2004)

Svetlana Kuznetsova

Russia
Birthdate: June 27, 1985
Birthplace: St. Petersburg, Russia
Height: 5' 9"
Weight: 161 lbs.
Plays: Right-handed
List of awards: 5 titles including 1 Grand Slam (US Open 2004)

Elena Dementieva

Russia
Birthdate: October 15, 1981
Birthplace: Moscow, Russia
Height: 5'11"
Weight: 141 lbs.
Plays: Right-handed
List of awards: 3 titles (no Grand Slam)

Roger Federer

Switzerland
Birthdate: August 8, 1981
Birthplace: Basel, Switzerland
Height: 6'1"
Weight: 177 lbs.
Plays: Right-handed
Pro since: 1998
Best ATP ranking: No. 1 (February 2, 2004)
List of awards: 20 singles, including 4 Grand Slam titles (Wimbledon 2003 and 2004, the Australian Open 2004, the US Open 2004)

Lleyton Hewitt

Australia
Birthdate: February 24, 1981
Birthplace: Adelaide, Australia
Height: 5'11"
Weight: 157 lbs.
Plays: Right-handed
Pro since: 1998
Best ATP ranking: 1
List of Awards: 23 singles, including 2 Grand Slam titles (US Open 2001 and Wimbledon 2002)

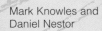

Mark Knowles and
Daniel Nestor

The Girls

Title Goes to Krajicek
She was only 15. The Netherlander Michaella Krajicek captured the first Grand Slam title in her short career. She brilliantly defeated the American Jessica Kirkland in two sets 6/1, 6/1. Richard could be proud of his stepsister.

The Boys

Monfils is Happy with a Small Slam
After winning the Australian Open, the French Open and Wimbledon, the French Gael Monfils could have claimed the Boys' Grand Slam. He was defeated in the third round by the Serbian Viktor Troicki, due to lack of preparation (after a knee injury that put him out of the courts for six weeks). It is thus the Scottish Andrew Murray, who took advantage of it and became the first Briton to win the US Open.

Women's Doubles

Kuznetsova Could Have Doubled the Bet

Hardly had she captured the first Grand Slam title in her career that the Russian Svetlana Kuznetsova had to gather the little strength she had left to play the women's doubles final. Unfortunately for her and her teammate, Elena Likhovtseva, there was nothing she could do against the world No.1 pair: Virginia Ruano Pascual and Paola Suarez. The latters gave themselves the pleasure of winning the third Grand Slam this year after the Australian and the French Open.

Women's Doubles Results

- V. RUANO PASCUAL / P. SUAREZ — 6-2 6-4
- J. HUSAROVA / C. MARTINEZ — 7-6(5) 3-6 6-2
  - V. RUANO PASCUAL / P. SUAREZ — 6-3 6-3
- E. DEMENTIEVA / A. SUGIYAMA — 6-2 6-4
- A. HUBER / T. TANASUGARN — 6-4 2-6 6-3
  - E. DEMENTIEVA / A. SUGIYAMA — 4-6 6-2 6-4
    - V. RUANO PASCUAL / P. SUAREZ — w.o*
- B. SCHETT / P. SCHNYDER — 7-6(6) 7-6(5)
- J. LEE / S. PENG — 4-6 6-1 7-6(9)
  - B. SCHETT / P. SCHNYDER — 6-2 7-5
- M. NAVRATILOVA / L. RAYMOND — 6-4 6-3
- S. KUZNETSOVA / E. LIKHOVTSEVA — 6-2 ab.
  - S. KUZNETSOVA / E. LIKHOVTSEVA — 6-7(6) 7-6(5) 6-1
    - S. KUZNETSOVA / E. LIKHOVTSEVA — 6-4 6-2
      - **V. RUANO PASCUAL / P. SUAREZ — 6-4 7-5**

The Mixed Doubles

The Russians Are Everywhere!

Winning these doubles with the American Bob Bryan, Mike's brother, comforted the Russian Vera Zvonareva, who was defeated in the fourth round of the singles' draw by Elena Dementieva. They defeated the seeded 1 Stubbs/Nestor in the semi-finals before winning over the pair Molik/Woodbridge (6/3, 6/4).

Mixed Doubles Results

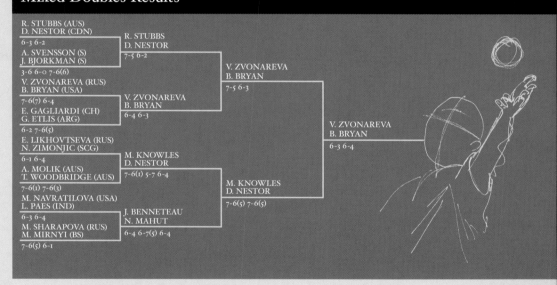

Men's doubles

And the Winners are...Knowles and Nestor

The pair formed by Mark Knowles (Bahamas) and Daniel Nestor (Canada) defeated the Indian Leander Paes and the Czech David Rikl. It is the second Grand Slam of their career. In semi-finals, they had defeated the French Nicolas Mahut and Julien Benneteau, who had themselves beaten the Bryan brothers.

Men's Doubles Results

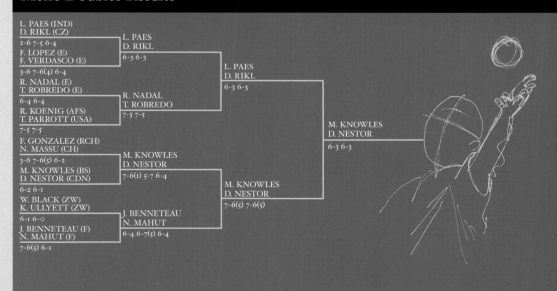

* walkover

Spain and the United States to the Final

In Alicante, the Frenchmen seemed to be paralysed in front of the overexcited Spaniards. The latter are now to face the Americans, who quickly defeated the Belarusians, in the final in the beginning of December.

Spain 4 – France 1

Location: Alicante (Spain)
Surface: red clay

The Frenchmen Were Given the Bulls' Part

Once again, the gifted Rafael Nadal was fantastic. He is the one who stopped France's hopes to reach the Davis Cup final they have been awaiting since their defeat in 2002 by Russia. Captain Guy Forget was very concerned in Alicante's Arenas. Who to choose for the singles match? While French No.1 Sebastien Grosjean put an end to his season, Forget preferred Paul-Henri Mathieu for the first match against Carlos Moya. In great shape for a few weeks, PHM played brilliantly and won a great five-set match: 6/3, 3/6, 2/6, 6/3, 6/3. France: one point. But the illusion was not to last long. Arnaud Clement's results had been catastrophic for some time. This is why Forget opted for Santoro for the second singles match. There was much at stake and he lost it all. Ferrero won over Santoro (6/3, 6/1, 1/6, 6/3). Furthermore, the latter's wrist was painful. Clement eventually replaced him next to Michael Llodra for the doubles. But the pair Nadal/Robredo defeated them 7/6, 4/6, 6/2, 2/6, 6/3. Spain was only one point from victory. Rafael Nadel humiliated Arnaud Clement 6/4, 6/1, 6/2 and made his country win. Nadal's eagerness will be a considerable asset against the Americans, in the final.

United States 4 – Belarus 0

Location: Charleston (United States)
Surface: hard court

Roddick Teased Once Again the Radar

Would the Davis Cup be a source of inspiration for him? Indeed, Andy Roddick improved once again his world fastest serve record. A record he already broke in the quarterfinals against Sweden. This time, the radar registered an incredible speed of 155 mph. At the end of the second day, the American already ensured their qualification for the final. Roddick quickly put Vladimir Voltchkov in difficulties and defeated him 6/1, 6/4, 6/4 in 1 hour and 33 minutes. Then, Mardy Fish captured the second point, winning his struggle against Max Mirnyi 7/5, 6/2, 3/6, 6/3. On Saturday, the twins Mike and Bob Bryan destroyed the pair Mirnyi/Skrypko 6/1, 6/3, 7/5. The world No. 2 has reached his first Davis Cup final without losing one single set since the beginning of the competition. The United States had not reached this stage of the competition since 1997. They will meet the Spaniards who defeated the Frenchmen in the other semi-final.

Andy Roddick, Bob Bryan, Mardy Fish and Mike Bryan

Opposite:
Tommy Robredo
and Rafael Nadal

Bob and
Mike Bryan

Results

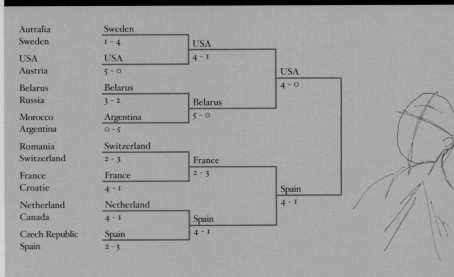

Autralia	Sweden			
Sweden	1 - 4	USA		
USA	USA	4 - 1		
Austria	5 - 0		USA	
Belarus	Belarus		4 - 0	
Russia	3 - 2	Belarus		
Morocco	Argentina	5 - 0		
Argentina	0 - 5			
Romania	Switzerland			
Switzerland	2 - 3	France		
France	France	2 - 3		
Croatie	4 - 1		Spain	
Netherland	Netherland		4 - 1	
Canada	4 - 1	Spain		
Czech Republic	Spain	4 - 1		
Spain	2 - 3			

Monfils The Great

The 18-year-old French Gael Monfils is ending the year
in the shoes of a World No. 1. He is the best of the boys.
Winner of three Grand Slams, he is now entering the
Men's competition. He hopes his star will still be shining
in the ATP Race.

Yes indeed, Gael Monfils is great. He is tall (6'4" for 170 lbs.),
but not only his size is high. The French Gael Monfils turned
18 on September 1, 2004, and he plays tennis. Better than
all the other boys on Earth as he ended the season with 3
Grand Slam titles. First of all, he won the Australian Open. It
was already enough to hear from him. But he remained cool:
"I saw the names of Andy Roddick or Rod Laver on the cup,
who are now pros, but some of the names are not in ATP
Tour." Then he claimed Roland-Garros title. As from then of
course, he becomes a topic of interest for Media.

But he remains realistic. "It is good to win in the junior competition; it is a good step forward. But I hope I will lift the Men's trophy within two or three years." Eventually he comes to Wimbledon to capture a third title. Monfils is one of only four players to have performed the Small Slam, and the first since Stefan Edberg in 1983. Only the fourth one is missing to achieve the Grand Slam. He failed in the third round of the US Open. However it is already great to have captured three junior Grand Slams in a year. But Gael remains quiet about all this. "Only people around me made a fuss about it, he confirms. For me, junior time is over, it is not important anymore. I know I am the 2004 junior world No. 1. But I want to go further."

Gael started playing tennis when he was four. His father, working for France Telecom, and her mother, working as a nurse, let him leave the home when he was 13 to join the 'Pôle France' in Reims and then the 'INSEP' (National Institute for Sport and Physical Education), where he was trained by Olivier Delaître, Louis Borfiga and Guillaume Marx. In September, he keeps in touch with the 'Fédération française de tennis' but joins the new group created by Arnaud Lagardère in the 'Paris-Jean Bouin Club'. Thierry Champion then becomes his new coach. In October, he is invited by Patrice Dominguez to take part in the 'Open de Moselle' to play his first ATP tournament. With a powerful Roddick-style serve and a killing forehand, he wins his first ATP match against the Belgian Xavier Malisse (3/6, 7/6 (7-4), giving up). He then received lots of compliments. Even Guy Forget is convinced: "His behaviour is very different from the other French but I like it. There was sometimes a shade of indifference in his attitude but he is a rough diamond. Thierry Champion will polish him and make him shiny. He is a nice rock!" But again, Gael is quiet and peaceful: "I am very pleased to be in the next round obviously, however this is not as if I had won the match. Xavier retired and I think if he had kept he still had good chances of defeating me. If I start thinking 'Great I won one match', I won't manage. Now I have to confirm." He confirmed the day after, by beating Olivier Patience, ranked 252 places above him in the world ranking. He is then defeated by Richard Gasquet.

It is a noticeable and noticed ATP start. Gael is optimistic, as well as hardworking. "I have to go on training hard and believing in what I am doing", he said. "And then if it works, that will be perfect! Otherwise it is not so serious! But there is no reason for my game to become bad in the Men's Race. If I can be junior No. 1, I should be able to be in the top 50, if I work hard." Maybe even in a higher top. In any case he entered the French Tennis History. From his point of view the most important is still to come.

> " For me, the junior period is over, it is not important anymore. I know I am the 2004 junior world No. 1. But I want to go further. "
>
> *Gaël Monfils*

ACKNOWLEDGEMENTS

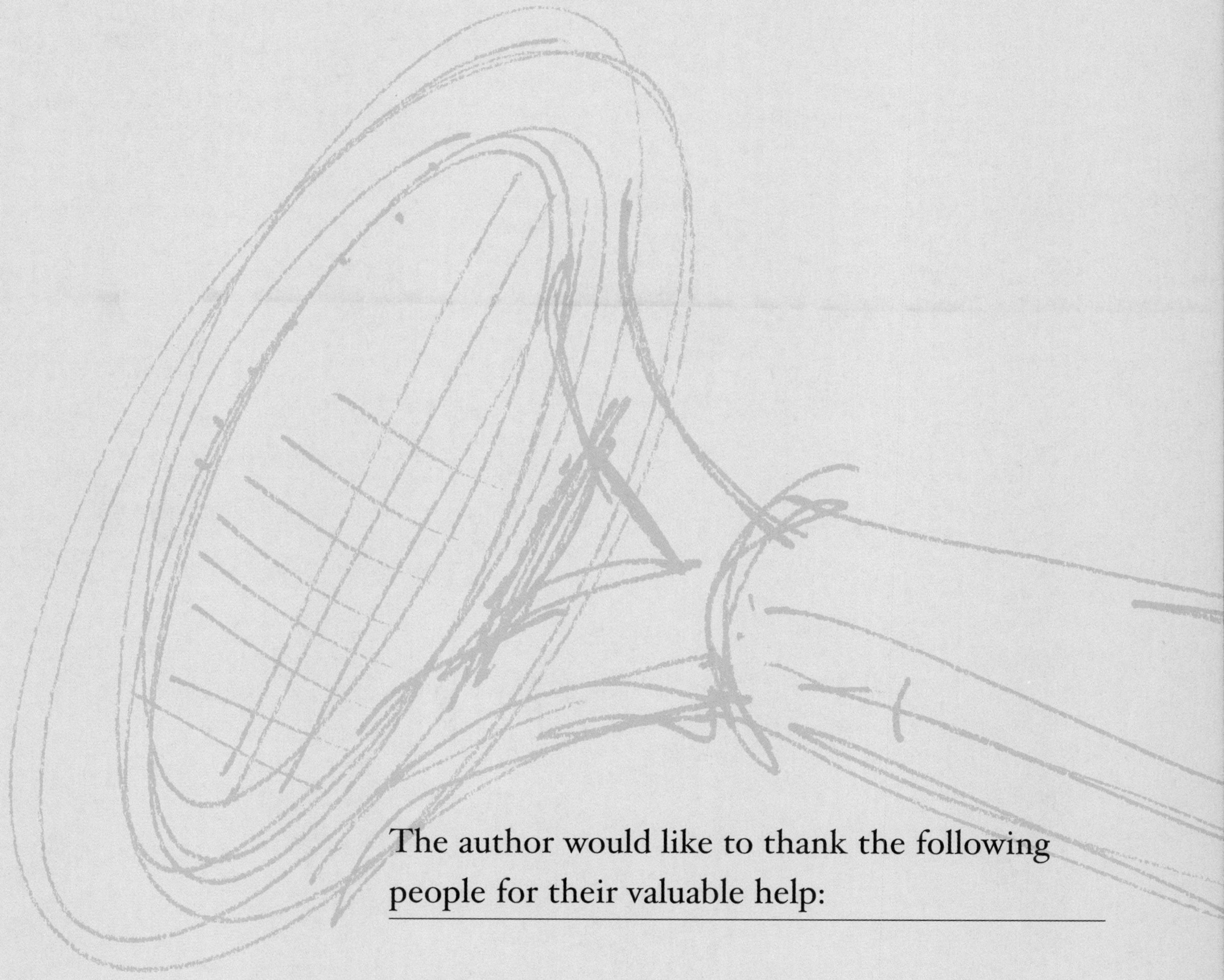

The author would like to thank the following people for their valuable help:

Marc Agboton

Cécile Delhez

Michael Fronin

Audrey Tartarat

Benjamin Deceuninck

Natacha De Roeck

Sabrina Favre